SCIENCE AND CULTURE SERIES

JOSEPH HUSSLEIN, S.J., Ph.D., GENERAL EDITOR

THE JESUIT IN FOCUS

THE JESUIT
IN FOCUS

JAMES J. DALY, S.J.

THE BRUCE PUBLISHING COMPANY
MILWAUKEE

Imprimi potest: GULIELMUS M. MAGEE, S.J., Praep. Prov. Chicagiensis
Nihil obstat: H. B. RIES, Censor librorum
Imprimatur: ✠ MOSES E. KILEY, Archiepiscopus Milwaukiensis

May 3, 1940

SOCIETATI
JESU
AMANTISSIMUS
1540 — 1940

AUTHOR'S FOREWORD

THE title of this book is a criticism of many popular sketches, sometimes caricatures, of the Jesuits. The variety of angles at which I look at my subject may give the chapters a scrambled and unassorted appearance; but I think they will be found to coalesce into a unity of impression which will be an honest and faithful representation of the Jesuits by one who is so fortunate as to have lived for fifty years in the Society of Jesus.

I have found the making of this book such a congenial employment that I feel grateful to Charles H. Cloud, S.J., for the suggestion which set me writing it. I wish to give special thanks to Leo A. Hogue, S.J., for his generously given help. Among those who cheerfully responded to calls for aid, I wish to mention gratefully William J. Young, S.J., John J. Wellmuth, S.J., C. A. Shyne, S.J., L. J. Kenny, S.J., and Francis S. Betten, S.J.

My thanks also to *America, Thought,* and the *Messenger of the Sacred Heart* for permission to reprint some of the chapters which appeared first in their pages; to the Oxford University Press for kindly allowing me to use two extracts from the letters and poems of Gerard Manley Hopkins and also one of his poems; to Sheed and Ward for G. K. Chesterton's poem; and to *America* for that of Eileen Duggan.

University of Detroit,
May, 1940

CONTENTS

THE JESUIT IN FOCUS

INTRODUCTION

L AUDED and maligned throughout the centuries, the Jesuits have ever been a mystery to many. So it was from the beginning of their Order.

They came at a time when England and the Continent of Europe were in a ferment of religious revolt. Five years earlier, and Henry VIII had assumed headship of the Church in England. Four years, and Calvin had established himself spiritual dictator in Geneva. Three years, and King Christian III by royal mandate made Lutheranism the religion of Denmark and Norway. One year, and Luther and Melanchthon, in a decision tremendously important as a presage of future events, had sanctioned the bigamy of Philip of Hesse. The dikes were broken; the flood had been let loose.

Then it was, in the hour set by Divine Providence, that the Jesuits made their appearance as a new Religious Order approved by the Church, their number officially limited to sixty men only — a limitation later removed.

Insignificant as such a force may seem, its members possessed the qualities of learning and leadership, together with complete devotion to their Captain Christ. Like the Israelites of old they wielded alike both trowel and sword. With one hand they built up or fortified anew the walls of the spiritual Jerusalem, while with the other they fought off the foe. Men like Faber and Canisius alone were worth more than whole battalions. And so, too, Lainez and Salmeron, when five years after the establishment of their Order the Council of Trent was called, at once proved to be unchallenged exponents of the Faith.

Small wonder, then, that these men were marked out for all the fierce attacks and studied calumnies of their enemies, who first and foremost were always the enemies of the Church! So it came about that before long a character purely mythical was attributed to them. War stories were manufactured then as they are concocted now, but with this difference in the instance of the Jesuits, that the war to be waged for Christ and for His Church never ended, and hence, too, the Jesuit myth has never died. They had made themselves conspicuous especially in their loyalty to Christ's representative on earth, and for that a double portion of the world's odium was their inevitable due. All the vials of its accumulated wrath were broken over their devoted heads. But for this, too, they had been prepared.

Time and again triumphantly refuted, the slanders against the sons of St. Ignatius continued to persist in plainly biased or purely secular literature and history. Handed down from century to century, the fiction grew by repetition. In the very lexicon of the English language it found a place at last wherein to crystallize its bias in just one single word: "Jesuitical!" A single word, but condensed in it were all the gall and bitterness of persecuting bigotry through the centuries.

Thus, under the Jesuit name was perpetuated the Jesuit myth. It was not one but many. Legion was its name. Duhr, the Jesuit historical scholar, was able to compile an entire modern Grimm's *Fairy Tales* in his own huge anthology of fables about the Jesuits,* which he once more took pains to refute.

Sensational as the Jesuit in fiction can unquestionably be made, yet the Jesuit in fact, depicted in this volume, may prove even more astonishing to those unacquainted with the ideals of the Religious Life. As the old saw has it, truth is often more strange than fiction.

The Jesuits most particularly referred to here are naturally those of our own times. In these the reader also will be espe-

---

* *Jesuitenfabeln.*

cially interested. Yet the picture presented of them will no less adequately serve to portray the Jesuits of any other period. The Society of Jesus has not changed within its four hundred years. It is the same in all essentials now as it was on that eventful day, September 27, in the year 1540, when the Basque Warrior-Saint, Ignatius of Loyola, knelt to receive from the hands of Pope Paul III the charter for his Company of Jesus. "The finger of God is here!" was the Pope's significant ejaculation.

A new work had begun within the Church. A new Religious Order had sprung into being, dedicated to the defense of the Holy See, and bound by special vow to carry out whatever the reigning Pontiff or his successors in the Chair of Peter might command "concerning the advancement of souls and the spreading of the Faith." These commands—understanding no sin to be involved—were to be executed by its members instantly, without evasion or excuse, "going to whatever country," the Bull of Institution reads, "into which they may send us, whether among the Turks or other heathen, and even to the Indies, or among whatever heretics and schismatics, or among any believers whomsoever" (*Regimini Militantis Ecclesiae*).

So, then, with the Sacred Name of Jesus flaming brightly on their standards, the sons of St. Ignatius pressed forward, age after age, century after century, with noble disregard of self, battling in the cause of God, driving their stakes and pitching their tents wherever the Vicar of Christ might call on them for service.

Though founded in the days of the Reformation, the Jesuits were never a mere defensive force. With Europe seething in rebellion against the center of Christendom, and with only a handful of followers at his command, St. Ignatius planned the spiritual conquest of the Holy Land, an undertaking quickly found impossible owing to circumstances abroad. But no such happenings foiled the mission of St. Francis Xavier. Without delay that most brilliant of university men and gifted natural genius was dispatched to the very ends of the earth to win them for Christ. Soon everywhere the Jesuits might be seen constructively at work: building universities, teaching children the rudiments of religion, founding new missions in all quarters of the globe, and establishing at home a system of higher education that became supreme in Europe. And all this was unfailingly directed, with sound Jesuit logic, to the "one thing necessary," as pointed out by Christ.

Whether drained in numbers by martyrdoms among the savage Iroquois, or weakened by pestilential fevers that swept the blazing sands of Africa, or racked and hanged and quartered by the Cecils of England and Elizabeth, yet their places were never left vacant. New recruits were eager to catch up the torches dropped from veteran hands, and in their strong and youthful grip to bear them onward. Decked with honors in the foremost centers of learning or pierced to death with arrows in the outposts of civilization, they never failed to keep their tryst with Christ wherever obedience bade them to be. Obedience, the signal virtue of their Order!

While account must be taken for human weakness, yet definitely it can be said that there is no obverse to this picture, such as writers like Macaulay unblushingly paint.

Then why those attacks on the Society of Jesus, even from within the Church, that actually led to its temporary suppression?

The answer can pithily be given by simply presenting to the reader another set of pictures quite similar: traitor, deceiver of the people, forbidding tribute to be paid to Caesar, usurper, wine bibber, Sabbath breaker, violator of God's commandments, spurner of the law, blasphemer, one possessed, "Do not we say well that thou art a Samaritan and hast a devil?" — Yes, it was of the Son of Man that all this was spoken.

And who were those responsible for these reproaches? Men of substance and reputation, leaders of His own people, spokesmen in the name of religion.

That His disciples would be treated in the same manner as

Himself, Christ was not slow to state: "The disciple is not above the master, nor the servant above his lord." And so He concludes: "If they have called the good man of the house Beelzebub, how much more them of his household? Therefore fear them not" (Matt. 10:24–26). Does that answer suffice?

What wonder, then, that in the case of the Society, as in the case of Christ, the princes of the people and those in high places plotted for her death and openly demanded it. To render to God the things of God, rather than to deliver them up to Caesar, was for these men — Catholics though they were! — an intolerable doctrine. And the Jesuits taught it. So the blow fell, with results unspeakably terrible for the interest of souls.

Yet even during the long, sad decades of its Suppression, the Society's life was never entirely extinguished. A spark of it lingered on under the ashes of humiliation in the then friendly Russia. It was to burst forth into new light with the Society's glorious Restoration. "Therefore fear them not."

Even the very name applied to its members — *Jesuita,* "Jesus-thus" — was given them in purest mockery. It was the white garment of Herod cast over their shoulders. But they accepted it, and with reverence have worn it ever since, like a consecrated chasuble. It expressed to them, not indeed something already achieved, a vaunt, a senseless brag — as their enemies applied it — but a goal to be kept in sight, the whole aim and purpose of their life, that so daily they might grow to be more like to Jesus, Son of Mary.

But what the reader rightly must demand here is documentary evidence. That, too, is promptly supplied in the immediately following chapters which deal with the Constitutions of the Society of Jesus and with the Ignatian Spiritual Exercises. The former are authentic witnesses to the Order's true nature, while the latter have rightly been called by Dr. Harvey the Jesuit's "Manual of Discipline."* The four weeks into which

---

* *Ignatius Loyola,* A General in the Church Militant. By Robert Harvey, M.A., B.D., D.Th., The Bruce Publishing Company, Milwaukee.

these Exercises are divided, can best be regarded as a realistic application to our own individual lives of the eternal verities of religion and of the lofty teachings of Christ. They are nothing else than the rich flowering of the Counsels, the Commandments, and the Sermon on the Mount.

A grasp of these facts will make it plain also why the Jesuit does not sacrifice his individuality. It is such a training precisely that strengthens character, develops in it all that is best, and burnishes into new brightness man's finest natural qualities. As a parallel — what personalities stand out in bolder contrast than those of Peter, the "Rock," and John, the "Son of Thunder"? Yet both men were taught in the one same school of Christ, responded to His words with every fiber of their being, and drank in at every glance the penetrating power of His Divine Presence. "We saw his glory, the glory as it were of the only begotten of the Father, full of grace and truth" (John 1:14). It is on this same Christ, disclosed to him by the written Gospels and tabernacled bodily under the same roof with him, that the Jesuit is taught to form himself, in the way that God designs.

Surely, then, there can be no mystery about the Jesuit. The mystery is in the blurred and spurious images that misrepresent him. It is the blur that mystifies, not the Jesuit. The remedy is to see him in focus.

We have thus cast what might be termed an aviator's quick glance out of the clouds, over the wide terrain of the Society's labors, sufferings, and achievements, as they swept away beneath us in our course. At the same time it has been possible to give at least a preliminary answer to certain salient difficulties that may have been in the reader's mind. With that, we trust, the sympathetic and intelligent approach to the following chapters has been facilitated.

JOSEPH HUSSLEIN, S.J., PH.D.
General Editor, Science and Culture Series

CHAPTER 1

THE JESUIT CONSTITUTIONS

THE publishers of a popular history of the Jesuits, which appeared some ten years ago, called it on the jacket "a true and unbiased account of the greatest secret society of all time." A Jesuit would know at once before reading the book that it was not true and unbiased if it warranted the publishers in describing the Society of Jesus as a secret society. The advertisement would have lost its force with any reader who turned to the bibliography printed at the end of the book. There the author listed among the books he had consulted every notable official document the Society has issued for its members during nearly four hundred years. The Constitutions, the Rules, Decrees of Congregations, Letters of the Generals, the *Monumenta Ignatiana,* whatever domestic literature a Jesuit has at his disposal for the formation of his Jesuit life, it is all there. Nothing is omitted.

In obtaining access to all these sources of information, the author was not obliged to have recourse to special ingenuity or to obtain special privileges. All he had to do was to consult the shelves of any large library. As the late Father Herbert Thurston pointed out in his article on the Jesuits in Hasting's *Encyclopaedia of Religion and Ethics,* the "Constitutions, privileges, and secret instructions which the Society has been accused of guarding so jealously from profane eyes are now to be found in every public library. On the many occasions when the Order has been expelled from the different cities and States of Europe, even apart from the general suppression of 1773, their books, manuscripts, and most secret papers have over and over again been seized. Many public collections contain hundreds of volumes of such impounded papers. The Jesuits must have been clever indeed, and their assailants the most bungling of police agents, if they always succeeded in destroying the evidence of the existence of an inner circle of initiates conspiring against the political and moral order of the world."

One wonders in what sense a Society, whose private and official papers for so long a period have been accessible to anyone caring to see them, can be said to be a secret society. And many prying eyes and inquisitorial minds have been busy at various times on these records in the hope of discovering grounds for the fantastic legends current in countries where political and sectarian parties have established a tradition of suspicion and hostility toward Jesuits. Consequently, without wishing in the least to indulge in hyberbole, I have no hesitation in saying that no organization of men, inside the Church or outside of it, is less secret in its constitutions and methods than the Society of Jesus.

It is not my purpose to give a detailed study or even an outline of the Constitution: that has been done often enough in various biographies of St. Ignatius and in popular books about the Society. The *Institute of the Society,* containing the Constitutions and Rules, is within easy reach of anyone who wishes to verify whatever is said about them. I shall here try to give some notion of the spirit that inspired and informs them.

In that great book, *The Development of Christian Doctrine,* which Newman wrote as he was about to step into the Catholic Church, he has one of those illuminating passages for which his genius is famous. Newman came to know Jesuits better in the years of his Catholic life, but there is no evidence that he ever experienced a change of mind in his brilliant generalization about the Society. "At length," he writes, "in the last era of ecclesiastical revolution, another principle of early Monachism, which had been partially developed, was brought out into singular prominence in the history of the Jesuits. 'Obedience,' said an ancient abbot, 'is a monk's service, with which he shall be heard in prayer, and shall stand with confidence by the Crucified, for so the Lord came to the cross, being made obedient even unto death'; but it was reserved for modern times to furnish the perfect illustration of this virtue, and to receive the full blessing which follows it. The great Society, which bears no earthly name, still more secular [than the older Orders] in its organization, and still more simply dependent on the See of Peter, has been still more distinguished than any other Order before it for the rule of obedience, while it has compensated the danger of its free intercourse with the world by its scientific adherence to devotional exercises. The hermitage, the cloister, the inquisitor, and the friar were suited to other states of society; with the Jesuits, as well as with the religious Communities, which are their juniors, usefulness, secular and religious, literature, education, the confessional, preaching, the oversight of the poor, the care of the sick, have been chief objects of attention; great cities have been the scene of operation; bodily austerities and the ceremonial of devotion have been made of secondary importance. Yet it may fairly be questioned, whether, in an intellectual age, when freedom both of thought and action is so dearly prized, a greater penance can be devised for the soldier of Christ than the absolute surrender of judgment and will to the command of another."

The obedience, which Newman notes as the characteristic virtue of Jesuits, is not readily understood and has been variously caricatured. It is usually described as military, a somewhat misleading epithet. Mr. Hendrik Van Loon, an American writer of popular treatises, in a recent book on art finds occasion, with the common run of art critics, to refer caustically to the Jesuits as the great patrons of rococo, and he goes on to say, as if in explanation and with innocent assurance, that the Jesuit Order is "a military organization rather than a religious institution." He forgot for the moment that military organizations seldom, if ever, favor rococo architecture. The military spirit does not feel impelled to express itself in armories, barracks and fortifications of flamboyant splendor.

It must be conceded that the association of Jesuit and military obedience is natural and not without some grounds. Obedience is pre-eminently a military virtue. St. Ignatius had been a soldier, and the name he gave his Society in its Spanish form is Company, suggesting a military unit. His Company was to be a sort of flying squadron, with detachments always ready to be dispatched by the Church wherever the conflict with error was most pressing. Elasticity, mobility, discipline and smartness in carrying out orders — all these desirable qualities inevitably conjure up pictures of an army in action. Moreover, in the meditations on the Kingdom of Christ and the Two Standards, St. Ignatius employs a few military terms to indicate the moral and spiritual warfare forever waging in the world under two opposing commanders, Christ and Lucifer.

On the other hand, it is to be remembered that St. Ignatius had been a soldier for only three years when he was wounded at Pampeluna. If he borrowed from a military vocabulary in giving a name to his Society and indicating its functions, he was doing nothing new or original. Ecclesiastical literature, from the Bible onward, had long familiarized readers with the comparison between spiritual conflicts and military actions. Such expressions as the "army of God," "a soldier of the Cross," "in battle array," were not new in the time of Ignatius. They were especially popular with the Protestant reformers of his day. If Mr. Van Loon wishes to find a perfect example of a religious organization which was a military institution, his search would be more promising if he turned his eyes to the Roundhead army of Cromwell.

The obedience practised by a Jesuit is considerably different from that in an army. In the first place, it is more human. It is more human because it is supernatural. And this is not pure paradox. But it is, and will continue to be, pure paradox, wholly unintelligble to persons who refuse to acquaint themselves with the Catholic idea of the supernatural, the kind of person who sees only hard fanaticism in the practice of penance.

In the Articles of War that "shall at all times and in all places govern the Armies of the United States," we read in Article 64: "Any person subject to military law who, on any pretense . . . wilfully disobeys any command of his superior officer, shall suffer death or such other punishment as a court-martial may direct." That is a grim law when a man has neither respect for nor confidence in his superior officer. It is military law and is enforced in every army everywhere and at all times. It is so different from the law of obedience in the Society of Jesus as to be grotesque.

In his Summary of the Constitutions, read at the beginning of every month in Jesuit refectories, St. Ignatius declares that it is the interior law of love imprinted in the hearts of men that is to help the Society in advancing the service of God rather than written constitutions. He all but apologizes for writing rules at all, counting it a necessity imposed by long usage but recommended by human reason and experience. After the outline of the aims of the Society had been approved by the Pope in 1540, St. Ignatius showed a certain reluctance in drawing up a definitive draught of the Constitutions. They were not completed in their present form till shortly before the Saint died in 1556 and did not become the written code of the Order till the meeting of the first General Congregation of the Society after his death.

I do not pretend to know the reasons why the Saint was so slow in formulating the rules governing the Society; but the fact on its face does not tell in favor of a military attitude of mind. It may have been that Ignatius wished to see the rules tested in action before they received their final form. It is true, he always laid special stress on obedience. His famous letter on that virtue, written to the Jesuits of Coimbra three years before his death, is read publicly together with the Summary of the Constitutions in Jesuit houses every month. But there is nothing in that letter or in the Summary to suggest the hard and peremptory obedience of a military machine.

In some respects, indeed, the perfect obedience desired by St. Ignatius is of a more thorough and exacting kind than that of the army. He wished conformity of understanding as well as of will. And here again we meet a paradox. He wished this perfection of obedience because it made ordinary obedience, that is, the conformity of will required by the vow, more easy; and more human for being supernatural.

Anyone who will read the eleventh Rule of the Summary will find little difficulty in understanding the paradox. This rule supposes that everyone who enters the Society loves Christ and wishes to walk in His footsteps; and that he believes the sanction of Christ's Vicar and the history of its saintly men warrant him in thinking that in the Society he will grow in the love of Christ and will find in the observance of its rules opportunities of proving that love and becoming Christlike. If the Society is what it professes to be, the Society of Jesus, it is doing, collectively and individually, the will of Christ. That divine Will is made manifest to the Society, first, through the Vicar of Christ, and, afterwards to each member of the Society, through the expressed will of its superiors. Every act of obedience is an act of love of Christ. The more difficult the obedience is, the better opportunity it affords of expressing love of Christ.

Everyone may not accept the religious truths on which this philosophy is built. But, once they are granted, as all Christians must grant them, there is nothing insane or fanatical in a Jesuit's obedience. It is wholly different, except in promptitude, from military obedience because it is inspired by love rather than fear and does not depend upon accidental loyalties for generous performance. The government of the Society resembles that of the Athenian Commonwealth as described by Pericles: "It is carried on, not by formal and severe enactments, but by the ethical character and spontaneous energy of the people."

The vocation of a Jesuit is to work for the salvation of souls in such a way as to advance in virtue himself. His own progress in spiritual perfection is logically prior to every other consideration if it is to be an effective instrument in doing God's work. He can expect his life and labor to be blessed only while he does God's will rather than his own. His only fear is the fear that, if he is slack on any occasion in the matter of obedience, he will be guilty, not of a grave sin necessarily — very few commands are given in the Society under pain of grave sin — but of a "great refusal" in ignoring an inspiration of heaven urging him onward in the road of perfection leading to close union with Christ. It is a great refusal because it lowers the temper of the will, throws the soul into slower gear, inclines it to a career of weak compromise and mediocre performance.

When Newman wrote that the Jesuit's obedience is "absolute," it should not be necessary to say that he used that word in the sense which his context obviously conveys. In the thirty-sixth Rule of the Summary, St. Ignatius, desiring to illustrate obedience in its perfection, employs two similes which for three or four centuries have been a great comfort to those who wished to believe the Society of Jesus is a sinister and unscrupulous body of men. I shall quote the Rule: "Let everyone persuade himself that they who live under obedience must suffer themselves to be carried and ruled by divine Providence in their Superiors, as if they were a dead body, which suffers itself to be borne to any place and to be treated in any manner whatever; or like an old man's staff, which serves him, who holds it in his hand, where and in what use soever he pleases."

The interpretation always placed upon this rule by wishful interpreters is that a Jesuit must be ready to commit any atrocity at the will of a superior: his conscience and common sense must have no play whatever. The introductory sentence of the rule should be a sufficient guard against any such reading. To a mind that is not somewhat unbalanced it will always be clear that divine Providence does not encourage us to the commission of atrocities and absurdities through any human agency whatever. In the thirty-first Rule, St. Ignatius had explicitly excluded the possibility of this interpretation when he says obedience is to be given "in all things where there appears no sin." And in his Letter on Obedience, he explains further the kind of blind obedience he has in mind. In the nineteenth paragraph of the Letter, he declares that the perfection of obedience does not hinder you, "if anything occurs to you different from the Superior's opinion, and it seems (after you have commended the same humbly to God) that it ought to be declared, but that you may propose it unto him," being ready to abide by any decision after representations have been made.

The two modifying clauses here quoted should prevent inhuman and fantastic concepts of Jesuit obedience. Mr. Henry Dwight Sedgwick closes his Life of St. Ignatius with a passage that seems to show a fairer attitude toward Jesuit obedience than has been customary outside the Church. He cannot avoid the military parallel but it may be allowed to illustrate his point: "The Constitution of the Order of Jesus can only be judged by those who are familiar with it in operation. It is less common, however, to find fault with the form and style of the Constitution than with its substance. Protestants have declaimed against what they call the iron constraint put upon the human soul. But if one stops to think, how does the Jesuit training differ, unless perhaps in conscientious intensity, from that of West Point or Saint-Cyr? In a military academy the whole weight of authority comes down on the individual soul. Substitute the flag for the cross, country for church, famous generals and marshals for saints and martyrs, honor for grace, and you will find that the constraint in either case is very much the same. Obedience is of equal obligation, the word of the superior as indisputable, the period of preparation about as long. As for liberty of thought, there is no more room for patriotic agnosticism in West Point than for religious agnosticism in a Jesuit college. In New York State men have been sent to prison for insult to the symbol of our patriotic faith. The difference is that we have lost our belief in supernatural religion, but not yet our faith in nationality. But whatever the plausibility of this comparison, there is, in truth, something humanly sacrilegious in coldly criticising a document, every clause of which was prayed over with tears, and offered to the Lord."

I think it happens comparatively seldom that a Jesuit feels any iron constraint in practising obedience. He is not in the field for honors and promotion, neither he nor his superiors. They have the same personal ends as himself, the same difficulties and private responsibilities. Indeed their responsibilities are greater because of their office. Even when their wish is hard to understand and hard to comply with, a Jesuit can suppose their wider outlook makes the decision a natural and wise provision. In any case, it is a good opportunity of practising a little penance and seeing just how much personal attachment one has for Him whose name the Society bears.

This frame of mind is the result of the "Spiritual Exercises" of St. Ignatius. The Constitutions of the Society are a sort of corollary of the Exercises and cannot be intelligible apart from them. For that reason, I shall devote the next chapters to a brief outline sketch of the nature and operation of the "Spiritual Exercises."

I have relegated to an appendix a detailed description of St. Ignatius's classic, "Spiritual Exercises." The reader, who wishes to have logical sequence at all costs, can satisfy his curiosity by turning at once to the end of the book. I shall attempt in the next four chapters to show the book in actual operation. My presentation of the Exercises in action, while more or less my own, will convey some understanding of the ground covered, and the stages of progress, in every retreat based upon the

Exercises. The variations in retreats are incidental and unimportant, and are only such as are to be expected from the diversity and individual characteristics of those who conduct retreats.

CHAPTER 2

MAKING A RETREAT

FIRST WEEK

JUST what are the mental and volitional experiences of anyone who makes the First Week of the Spiritual Exercises of St. Ignatius, that is, the first of the four parts into which they are divided? What are the successive steps and what the landing place before he takes off for the Second Week? What sequence of ideas occupies his mind? What is the nature of their impact upon his will?

Before I begin the Retreat itself, I am asked to consider a few fundamental truths. St. Ignatius calls this introductory step the Foundation. The purpose is to clear the landscape of the clutter of mundane objects which hem me about and spoil vision and perspective.

I have always thought that I was Tom or Dick or Mary or Jane, living at 40 Brownleaf Avenue, where the postman delivered my letters and I received my friends. Now I see — of course, I knew it all along, but not much more than subconsciously — I see, when I stop to consider, that the question of where I live is not the simple and commonplace matter I thought. I feel some of the astonishment and awe felt by the non-Catholic Robert Louis Stevenson when he shook himself loose momentarily from parochial overcrowding and took a look around:

"We inhabit a dead ember swimming wide in the blank of space, dizzily spinning as it swims, and lighted up from several million miles away by a more horrible hell-fire than was ever

17

conceived by theological imagination. Yet the dead ember is a green, commodious dwelling-place; and the reverberation of this hell-fire ripens flower and fruit, and mildly warms us on summer eves upon the lawn. Far off on all hands other dead embers, other flaming suns, wheel and race in an apparent void; the nearest is out of call, the farthest so far that the heart sickens in the effort to conceive the distance. Shipwrecked seamen on the deep, though they bestride but the truncheon of a boom, are safe and near at home compared with mankind on its bullet. Even to us who have no other it seems a strange, if not an appalling, place of residence."

And so I take myself out of the file where custom and convention have docketed and indexed me. I give myself a more realistic and far more impressive background, and put myself in the mood to study my case with a stern realism seldom reached in the petty urgencies of everyday life.

Here I am, then, on the back of a great flying bullet in a wilderness of space. How comes it I am here? And why? This is no time for spinning subtle speculations or blindfolding conscience or playing nice academic games. The normal man agrees with Lord Kelvin: "Overwhelming proofs of intelligence and benevolent design lie around us, showing us through nature the influence of a free will, and teaching us that all living beings depend upon one overacting Creator and Ruler."

God created the universe with its planets and flaming suns. He created this flying bullet and He created me and my immortal soul and put me on it. Why? He is omniscient and all-wise; He is not vague and purposeless; nothing in His Universe is too small to elude His infinite attention. Why did He put me here? He certainly did not put me here to forget about Him, to spend my life trying to discover reasons for doubting about His existence, to find fault with Him, to be indifferent about His wishes concerning me, doing as I please and in general disgracing Him. I am surely a disgrace to Him if I think and speak and act as if He had nothing at all to do with me or with the world He put me in, or thought of Him only casually now and then as of an uncomfortable acquaintance I was not eager to cultivate or to meet. If this be so, I must make Him, as I may put it in human language, ashamed He made me: a poor specimen, indeed, of the Divine craftsmanship which made me in His own image to reflect some of His moral beauty, purity, and holiness. And, if I disgrace Him this way, it does not matter whether I become a great artist, a great scientist conferring boons on the whole of mankind, or any other kind of benefactor or personage: I remain a disgrace to Him. For I have spent my whole life boasting that I can get along without Him while all along everything I had came from Him and depended upon Him. If this is not disgracing Him, and disgracing myself, then undutiful sons and daughters are no disgrace to anybody and are the happiest and noblest people in the world.

My reason tells me it would not be right to deny or forget that God is my Creator and sovereign Lord: if I acknowledge that He is, I praise Him. It tells me that there is never a time or circumstance that would absolve me from the stain of dishonor and dishonesty if I withheld from Him recognition of His supreme importance in His universe and in my life: if I never fail to give Him this recognition, I reverence Him. Finally, reason tells me that it would be outrageous to disobey Him: if I am always regardful of His wishes, I serve Him. And so I conclude that I was put on this flying bullet to praise, reverence, and serve Him.

Both reason and observation tell me that the perfection characteristic of rational beings is wrought by fidelity to this triple duty of praising, reverencing, and serving God. It brings out the best that is in us; it realizes our best self, the highest aspirations human nature is capable of. The most exalted instances of human perfection became such by making this triple duty the foremost obligation in life, the source and foundation of all duty. The faithful performance of it makes for the peace of nations and the noblest form of happiness. Indeed, we were created for perfection and for that which perfection brings, happiness, by giving God the praise, reverence, and service which are His due.

This is the way to give glory to God; glory may be defined as praise with reverence and service. Whatever process the reason employs, whether working to a conclusion from the side of God or from the side of my own nature, it tells me that I was created to give glory to God. God's infinite happiness does not need any glory I may give Him, but my own happiness does; my happiness in this world and in the world to come. My happiness in this world may be a sickly growth, overlaid with earthly sorrow, disappointment, pain, and failure; it will not be in full flower until such time as it is transplanted and blooms in the fields of eternity, forever fair, forever uncloying, a perfect thing pleasing to itself because it pleases Him who made it.

This is meant in saying that I was made to praise, reverence, and serve God in this world and thus save my soul. This is the answer to the question I ask when I stop to look at the wonderful place in which I find myself and wonder why I am in it.

The next question is: What about the rest of the universe, animate and inanimate creation, the events and happenings of the world, the circumstances in which I live and act, the external contacts I make with the world about me, my opportunities and drawbacks, my natural advantages and disadvantages, my trials, my failures, my successes, all the countless things, little and big, that I have to deal with in fashioning my life and shaping my course through the world from childhood to my dying day? God has either created them or permitted them so that out of them I can draw material with which to give Him glory. By His Divine will they are here not without an ultimate purpose, the only ultimate purpose they can possibly have, to give Him glory. As far as they affect me, they must give Him glory through me. They must be encountered by me as so many occasions for giving God praise, reverence, and service. God has arranged everything to give me a chance to make myself a credit to Him, thus glorifying His arrangement. The pleasant things I must use with moderation; the unpleasant I must meet with patience, fortitude, and resignation to His will. I can go along with what comes to me just so far as it helps me to grow in my union with God's will: when that is imperiled, I must break with the endangering thing no matter how violent the wrench. Be it fair weather or foul, I must have only one way of looking at it: fair is foul if it blows me out of my course, and foul is fair if it drives me to my Divinely appointed goal.

These truths recommend themselves to the normal reasonable man; they must be firmly grasped before the Retreat proper begins with the first meditations on sin.

Sin is a deliberate misuse of creatures, of opportunities of displaying my fidelity to my Creator. Sin has become such a familiar thing to us that, except in a few instances obviously horrible, it seldom impresses the mind and imagination for what it is, the most fearful thing in life. We must go to Divine revelation for enlightenment. Holy Scripture tells how some of the Angels, still in a state of probation, misused their liberty and intelligence by declining to give God the praise, reverence, and service that were His due. It does not sound grievous to our dulled ears. It was a sin, yes, but what is a sin? Well, look at what it did. It blasted Angelic beauty and darkened Angelic intelligence and changed Angelic loveliness and decorum into a turbulent hell of anguish and blasphemy. Again, Holy Scripture tells of what befell when our first parents sinned. They deliberately set aside the arrangements of their Creator, consulting their own devices and ambitions, and immediately havoc and misery swept down upon their souls and upon the peaceful earth which was never again to know the peace and security of primeval innocence. One sin can do that, and can I say lightly, "Oh, what is one sin more or less"? It is possible that a soul is suffering eternally on account of a single un-repented sin.

If God were not Infinite Love Itself, we should be tempted to think He was cruel. It is sin that is cruel and malicious. It is vicious enough to paralyze, so to speak, Divine Love, to make omnipotent Love helpless toward it. Uncontrite sin writes its own doom. Sin is bad enough when it defies a whole city or a whole nation or the whole world; but, when it defies the in-finite Creator, it reaches heights of malice which suggest un-thinkable depths of condemnation. I can only thank Christ, nailed to a cross for love of me, that I have been spared to come to my senses and to be sorry for the sins I have com-mitted. As I review my life, I am stricken at my callous indiffer-ence to the rights of my Creator and to the outpourings of His love for me.

Hell is not a pleasant subject: but it must be faced unflinch-ingly. As has been said, it is better to go to hell in this life than in the next. It has been Divinely revealed, and even cold reason gropes for something very much like it. Carelessness with a physical law, say, the law of gravity, when one is standing on the brink of a precipice or the roof of a towering office building, even when the carelessness is inadvertent, is sometimes visited with an appalling penalty: and no one says that anybody is cruel. The deliberate violation of a much more important law, a moral law, must have some inconceivably harsher penalty attached to it. At least, the reason does not leave us entirely unprepared for the existence of that eternal fire which the gentle Christ discloses as the abode of unrepented sin. I do not want to praise, reverence, and serve God because I am afraid of hell; but, if my sense of what is due Him should become blunted, if the love I ought to have for Him should cool, then I beg for the grace that the fear of hell shall hold me back when I am tempted to offend Him.

When death comes — how inevitable it is! — and my day is done, and I appear before my Judge, may my record of praise, reverence, and service be not too shameful to win a merciful hearing. If God had not come down to become a man like me, to suffer and die for me, and to merit for me, what a plight I should be in! What a desolate place this flying bullet would be!

CHAPTER 3

MAKING A RETREAT

SECOND WEEK

WHEN I enter the Second Week, I am keenly aware of my dismal performance in the primal duty of doing what God wanted me to do when He put me on this planet. I knew all along what He wanted, but in a sort of self-induced anesthesia. I was a romanticist, willfully closing my eyes to realities which might prove unpleasant. For, if there are two realities which everywhere impress the natural vision of a sojourner on our planet, they are the reality of God and the reality of sin. Newman's description of the world has now a new poignancy: "Starting then with the being of a God (which, as I have said, is as certain to me as the certainty of my own existence . . .) I look out of myself into the world of men, and there I see a sight which fills me with unspeakable distress. The world seems simply to give the lie to that great truth (that there is a God) of which my whole being is so full; and the effect upon me is, in consequence, as a matter of necessity, as confusing as if it denied that I was in existence myself. If I looked into a mirror and did not see my face, I should have the sort of feeling which actually comes upon me when I look into this living, busy world, and see no reflection of its Creator. . . .

"To consider the world in its length and breadth, its various history, the many races of man, their starts, their fortunes, their mutual alienation, their conflicts; and then their ways, habits, governments, forms of worship; their enterprises, their aimless courses, their random achievements and acquirements, the impotent conclusion of long-standing facts; the tokens so faint and broken of a superintending design; the blind evolution of what turn out to be great powers or truths; the progress of things, as if from unreasoning elements, not toward final causes; the greatness and littleness of man, his far-reaching aims, his short duration, the curtain hung over his futurity; the disappointments of life, the defeat of good, the success of evil, physical pain, mental anguish, the prevalence and intensity of sin, the pervading idolatries, the corruptions, the dreary, hopeless irreligion, that condition of the whole race, so fearfully yet exactly described in the Apostle's words, 'having no hope and without God in the world' — all this is a vision to dizzy and appall, and inflicts upon the mind the sense of a profound mystery, which is absolutely beyond human solution."

As we all know, the Cardinal finds the solution in the presence of sin in the world. "The human race is implicated in some terrible aboriginal calamity. It is out of joint with the purposes of its Creator." What is to become of me, caught as I am in this tremendous catastrophe? I am a poor, weak thing pitted against the enormous forces around me and the violent passions within me. What can I do in this vast spiritual maelstrom sucking me down into the depths?

In the preliminary meditation on the "Kingdom of Christ," the simple question is put to me: What would you do if a capable leader appeared, setting himself against the triumphant cohorts of sin and confusion, calling on all similarly minded men to follow him, and promising them victory in what to all appearances was a hopeless cause? In such a hypothesis, there can be, of course, only one answer. And then I realize that there is actually such a Leader in the world, who can offer me infinitely greater assurance of victory than any imaginable human leader. The disorder I see around me and in me is more than human mind and skill, be they never so eminent, can cope with. It requires a Divine deliverer, and a Divine deliverer there is. He calls me in person to range myself on His side, with all that is good and pure and noble in the world, and to help Him to restore God's primacy of truth, justice, and beauty to the world and to my soul. He Himself is God. Because He loved me, He assumed a human nature, my human nature, to redeem me from the bondage of sin and to show me by His example what glorious heights of moral and spiritual beauty my nature forfeited when sin came into this world.

And, now that my allegiance is pledged to Him, I proceed to study His human life from the Angel's announcement of His coming to the end of His active mission among the people, watching in reverent contemplation as they pass before me every word and act of His, and even conjecturing His thoughts and motives as He went on His way through life. Now I see, as I never saw before, the mighty import of the Annunciation. Only when the mind is filled with the awful plight of mankind, does the mystery take on full significance. What event in the history of the world can compare with it? No wonder the church in Catholic countries rings its bells three times a day, at morning, noon, and twilight, to ask the world to pause a moment in its occupations and to recall that supreme event which turned in our favor the tide of that awful battle between hell and Heaven for the souls of men. The battle had long been lost, and the loss had been final, were it not for this moment.

The world, which has forgotten Christ and His Mother, and often hates both, gives us a pale imitation of the Angelus when it asks us to stand uncovered and in silence for a minute to pay reverence to an earthly hero. But neither in our crowded city streets nor in the peaceful countryside of nations alienated from the Faith, is the *Angelus* bell heard. And, if it were, it would too often be regarded as a superstitious survival of a backward age, when the tempo of life was slower and duller and men had not yet come into the rich heritage of modern science.

As I contemplate Christ while the scenes of His early life pass before my inner eye, He speaks to me in the other persons of the mysteries as well as in His own Person; He speaks to me in the setting of the scene, in the episodes, in His very silence. I behold Him creating the atmosphere of a spiritual life; giving me, so to speak, the "hang" of it. It is strangely beautiful to watch and ponder over. And then St. Ignatius interposes with his meditation on "Two Standards." This famous meditation gathers up all the thoughts, impressions, feelings, and impulses which I have been experiencing into a concrete formula, giving them definition and direction, testing their worth by their reaction to a practical proposition.

The meditation of "Two Standards" gives me a clue which helps me to trace the seething confusion of the world and my own soul to the operation of a simple and easily intelligible law, the law of the Master of Iniquity; and presents in equally simple terms the only law that can hope to cope with the triumphant march of sin and disorder. The subtleties of Satan are reducible to such a commonplace formula that we are surprised at the variety and ease of its success. His instruction to the agents of temptation are at first to seduce the soul with dreams of riches (material, intellectual, any kind), fame, and power. There is question here of innocent dreams which cannot alarm the most sensitive conscience. Gradually these dreams will take possession of the soul, overmastering and dominating it, until they are realized, when the soul revels in the conscious enjoyment of its own power. A deadly sort of pride hands the soul over signed and sealed to the fellowship of Evil in this world and the next. And it may be noted, even when the dreams of fame and power are balked, they have already engendered a killing pride in the soul which often gives itself into Satan's hands in a mad despondency.

The inscription on Christ's Standard runs counter to that on

Satan's. He instructs His Angels and human lieutenants to persuade men of the real value of mortal fame and power, how transitory and worthless they are, perishable gauds extremely dangerous to the soul and its eternal interests. See how He Himself despised them. As long as I fasten my gaze upon Him, I have no trouble in understanding that worldly fame and power are almost ridiculous things in the business of realizing my best self, of pursuing spiritual aims, of glorifying my Creator, of following Christ, my Leader, in His warfare with the powers that beleaguer my soul and the souls of all men. I will have done with my dreams of fame and riches and honor. Help, my Divine Master, help me to desire with You poverty and obscurity, and, if it can be without sin, help me to court the contempt of the world in humble emulation of You, Divine Lover of my soul.

I have not spent these days in prayer and quiet self-communion without becoming aware that a cardinal decision challenges my will power. Either as regards the choice of a state of life or, if that is fixed, as regards a change of some kind in my conduct; there is a Rubicon to be crossed, there are bridges to be burned. The road forks here into two; one, leading to the side of the battling Christ; the other, to a less heroic station and less exacting performance. It is a critical moment and tries my manhood. If I do not rise to the stature of the graces and generous impulses of the soul now, I shall condemn my future to a demoralizing mediocrity and, perhaps, eternal loss. The memory of my partial recreancy will not be an inspiring feature in the days ahead; it will remain to cool my ardor, to temper my attachment to Christ, and to make life perplexing in a series of petty compromises with selfishness and the world.

To clarify the issue and to put some iron into my will, St. Ignatius asks me here to consider the "Three Classes" of men, faced with the necessity of acting in a crisis like mine. A large sum of money is involved. They made it, as men do, without any thought of God, and naturally are attached to it. Now it dawns on them that their attachment may not be good for their souls. The First Class would like to get rid of the attachment, but do nothing whatever about it. The Second Class are ready to do everything except yield possession of the money. The Third Class are prompt and ready to give up the money as God's service requires: whether they renounce it or retain it, is all the same to them; whichever God wants.

I can see, of course, that, if I am to throw in my lot with Christ's, my attitude should not be one of bartering and haggling, "dickering" for an advantage here and an advantage there, compounding with my selfishness, saying: "Give me what I want: with that, I will serve God"; keeping a shrewd eye on my own comforts and earthly interests while consulting the interest of God and my immortal soul. That is not the attitude of an ardent lover of Christ.

Still another consideration is called to my attention by St. Ignatius, helping to make clear to myself my present attitude toward Him whom I have chosen as my Leader and under whose standard I have wished to be enrolled. He describes three grades of the relationship I can choose as a creature to his Creator. He calls them the three Degrees of Humility, because humility is a virtue that rests on a true sense of my place in the universe.

The first degree is necessary for salvation: I am resolved to submit to God whenever a refusal would involve grave sin. With this degree, I may sometimes sin grievously through frailty. The second degree is higher: it is my firm purpose never to offend God at all. In this frame of mind, it is possible that I may sometimes commit a venial sin. The third and highest degree goes beyond any searching to see whether sin, mortal or venial, is involved, whether there is a law or not to ascertain how far I can go. I am not interested in "police regulations," so to speak, in order to save my skin or have a clean record. The third degree is that happy state when a lover of Christ wants to be like Him, not negatively by merely avoiding sin, but positively by liking what He liked, abhorring what He abhorred, making Christ's way of living and pleasing God his way. If I have this degree, I should be ashamed to have comforts and honor and worldly esteem: they would make me look too much unlike my King and Leader: how could I ever express my deep attachment to Him by having everything I wanted? Love, not law, is my controlling motive.

With thoughts such as these, I make the other meditations of the Second Week, studying Christ in His public life from His appearance at the Jordan to Palm Sunday, learning more and more the infinite depth of Divine love and kindling an answering fire in the cold embers of my heart. "Wherefore," says St. Ignatius, "let everyone be convinced that he will make progress in all spiritual matters in proportion as he shall have divested himself of his own self-love, his own will, and self-interest."

CHAPTER 4

MAKING A RETREAT

THIRD WEEK

I HAVE covered much ground by the time I come to the Third Week. I have not reached the peak of the Exercises, but I have won a lofty lookout from which the peak becomes visible and accessible. It seems a long time since I translated the idly accepted formula, that I was created to know, reverence, and serve God and thus save my soul, into a living truth, a supreme instance of realism importunately clamoring for my immediate and serious attention. I began to see what it meant to sin deliberately. I saw the baseness, cowardice, and injustice of sin, and the havoc it works in the world and in my own soul. Sin is the mighty discord, the great disorganizer: its issue is hardness of heart, remorse, degradation, hatred of the good, blindness of soul: its destiny and its natural affinity is the eternal abode of lost souls fixed forever in their piteous and awful attitude of defying the Creator. Sin has even lit those purifying and searching fires that saved souls willingly endure to be rid of its last traces before their admission into the timeless companionship of the purest and noblest.

I am not left to myself in the weary and endless struggle which mankind has to wage against its lower self, that corrupt self which the Enemy of men is allowed to play against my higher nature and destiny. It is more than a man's work: it is a God-man's work. They foolishly underrate the warfare who think it is not. We are the captains of our soul, but we need

compasses and charts and stars and many things besides a stout
heart, which only a higher Captain can give us. We need a
sound soul in the first place, and our King and Captain, Christ,
gave us that when He redeemed us. It no doubt sets a man up
and gives him a glow of satisfaction to write a blustering poem
or a smug essay on self-reliance: and it is not a hard thing to
do. But it is the silliest kind of whistling in the dark and must
make the judicious grieve. The proud pose of literary de-
claimers is rather ridiculous in a world like this, much more
ridiculous than that of the "proud prelate" they are so fond of
describing.

My King and Captain is Christ. I need Him, and He has
arranged His world in such a way that He needs me. He is
the Lord God of armies. His armies are recruited in a sinful
world from among those who are drawn to Him by every
high instinct in their fallen nature, by His forgetfulness of
Self in their behalf, by His urgent entreaties, by His valor in
what for me would be a hopeless cause and losing fight if He
were not there. No leader of men has ever attracted the love,
loyalty, and devotion that He has been able to win and keep.
The more I watch Him, the more I love Him. I want to be like
Him a little. I would like to have His ideas about the world
and God and eternity and the soul of man. I would like to
make His values my own. I would like to have some of His
disdain — it was not so much disdain as utter and unconscious
obliviousness — of all those things which my lower self makes
much of: fame and honor, riches and power, bodily well-being,
comforts and satisfactions, which put the soul to sleep and make
it the laughingstock of its enemies. And, most amazing and
mysterious of all, He loves me, loves me enough to die for me.

I should hate to think of Christ battling for His own in the
world and looking to me for help while I sit back and, consulting only my mean and selfish advantages, decline to join
Him in the one cause worth fighting and dying for. Joining
Him means imitating Him, burning all my bridges, those

little bridges leading back to the solaces so dear to human nature when it is weary of spiritual effort. If I love Christ, I will do this. I think I do love Him. But I am afraid of myself. My only surety is to love Him more, to beg for the grace of loving to the degree that it will be sheer happiness to suffer anything for no other reason than to be like Him.

If on the first Good Friday Christ's friends made merry or took their ease somewhere in a safe spot, any decent person would be shocked. It would disgust us to hear that they took their meals as usual that day and were not sick with grief. It is one of the human traits that mark us as not wholly degenerate, that we cannot enjoy life if one whom we love is in acute distress, that we actually find relief if we can suffer with him or are allowed the blessed privilege of self-sacrificing attendance upon him. I understand now why the saints and all great lovers of Christ were so hard on themselves.

I cannot help stopping to reflect on the denseness of good minds, ordinarily lucid enough, when they are turned on simple Catholic phenomena. Nothing is commoner in the world of literature than to see a puzzled bewilderment at the penitential practices of religious persons. The non-Catholic writer will grant, of course, that denying oneself now and then in little things is a habit which recommends itself to sound psychology as a means of developing character and increasing the sum total of happiness. But this obviously was not the object of St. Francis of Assisi and his kind. St. Simon Stylites did not live on top of a pillar to improve his character or to preserve a relish for such pleasures as the world has to offer. Whenever he thinks he can, the unbelieving writer will try to explain it by saying that the Saint was a fanatic or morbidly unnatural, and will class him with the fakirs of India, low types who for a living or from some repulsive eccentricity seem to find an animal satisfaction in self-inflicted tortures.

I do not know what motives impel a fakir to pass his life

in fearful penances, what grotesque and cruel gods he may be propitiating, what dark spirits may be possessing him. It is my ignorance and the terror of his nightmare idols and temples which make him an object of repulsion to me. But, if I knew it was out of hatred for sin and temptation, and out of love for all that was good and true and beautiful as embodied in the Divine Person of Christ that he condemned himself to a living death, I should have no trouble in saluting him reverently and kissing his feet. He would cease to be a dreadful caricature of holiness.

What appears to so many intelligent men as foolishness in the saints is sweet wisdom to me: it is the complete absence of all calculation and petty considerations in offering themselves to Christ for love of Him and all that He stands for. God made this fair material universe and He made it and all the fair things in it for the use and pleasure of men. It is not the material universe which has been blackened and perverted by sin, but only the soul of man so that he now is prone to use good things perversely. We need not look askance at God's bountiful gifts; but we have to look very much askance at ourselves. We have put ourselves in that perverse state where God's very gifts tend to hide Him from us. Christ lived here for thirty-three years and had little use of what we call the good things of life. Yet it was He who made them. He taught us that not by bread alone does man live; that there are better things than bread, and a higher life that mere bread cannot nourish. As we are now, we can often honor best the good things that God made by not using them. It is no discourtesy to the Creator to renounce His good gifts if we renounce the good for the better. What more exquisite gifts has He offered us than the renunciations of love in the companionship of Christ?

When the Third Degree of humility was first proposed to me, it seemed a too dizzy height for human nature to scale. Deliberately to prefer infirmity to sound health, the contempt of men rather than their respect, poverty above riches, even if I could give no more glory to God that painful way than if I were strong, famous, and wealthy, this seemed at first irrational, as if the misfortunes of life were in themselves desirable. But I quickly saw that the motive for the heroic choice made it less inhuman and took away all the appearance of unreasonableness. I was to choose these hard things, not because they were in themselves better than the pleasant things, not even because they were as good, but because they were the things that Christ chose. He made them His familiars. The cross had been a thing of disgrace and horror: He made it a symbol of love, honor, and beauty. He made Himself an outcast; and, ever since, His Church has been canonizing, and even mankind at large has been admiring, those who have made themselves outcasts for the love of Him. All the saints ardently desired to be outcasts like Christ; if honors came to them, they were an aggravation of earthly misery. St. Louis, the king, and St. Thomas Aquinas, the brilliant scholar, must have squirmed at the deference they received when they thought of Him whom they loved, the Man of sorrows and infirmities.

If I am to keep the stern purposes I made in the Second Week at the sticking point, and to shore up a feeble edifice till it settles and hardens and becomes firm against wind and weather, I see that what I need is greater and ever greater love of Christ. Meditation on Christ's passion ought to increase my love for Him to the degree that I shall shrink instinctively from being esteemed and made much of by a world that accounted Him of no importance except as a criminal to be done away with as ignominiously as possible.

I do not know how it was that Christ could suffer as He did during the Passion, since He was God as well as man. It is not necessary for me to know. All I know is that He suffered. He was Truth incarnate, and could not conceivably be merely going through the motions of one who was suffering as I would have suffered myself if I were in His place. His sweat of blood,

His agonized eyes, His exhaustion, quivering sinews torn by nails, anguish and death throes, were not theatrical counterfeits of a terrible reality. If His Godhead were allowed to act at all, it was only to intensify His torment. He was of finer fiber, more sensitive nerves, a soul that loathed sin and its hellish frenzies, unable to take merciful refuge, as we can, in the ignorance of what the next minute will bring of new agony.

I am to keep in mind that Christ was not suffering for a vague posterity, as we say that something or other will benefit future generations. Christ did not die for abstractions or address Himself to the masses. When He saw large masses, He saw them individually. In the only sense that is true, He suffered and died for me. Each of us can truthfully say that. He actually died for love of me. I was always in His Divine mind. He did it as much for me as if I were the last man and only man left upon the planet. Moreover, I must remember that He willed every pang that stabbed Him. He was not a helpless victim. He submitted as a lamb led to slaughter; but it was a Lion that submitted. Christ need not have summoned legions of Angels to rescue Him. Imagine what paralyzing consternation would have seized His tormentors if He had made them realize, as He could, that they were ill-treating their omnipotent Maker, the Creator of the universe.

When I look at Christ in His Passion, I see vividly the nature of sin and the nature of him who, as the enemy of my soul, introduced sin into God's world. It is the nature of sin, and of the father of sin, to defile, degrade, and tear to bits all the true goodness and loveliness in this world. The tempter can make himself appear gentle or charming or kindly or beautiful or heroic, so that his name has almost ceased to be hated among men; but I cannot but see now that he is "the most horrible object in creation, one who, if allowed, could reduce us to ashes by the very hideousness of his countenance, or the odor of his breath." What Divine fortitude it took on the part of Christ to come down from His pure heights and to put Himself in the power of His vile rebel angel! And why? Only to rescue me from that ruthless domination. My Redeemer, what is there I can do for You? You look very lonesome on Your Cross. If You have generous lovers anywhere, surely this is the place for them to gather.

It is clear that the Third Week disposes the soul for the highest union with God, even for mystical union if God be pleased to grant that great favor. The soul yearns to be one with Christ in His union with God. "I live now, not I, but Christ liveth in me." The following Week takes the illumined soul, filled with the interior Spirit of Christ, up to the ineffable Throne of Love and Light.

CHAPTER 5

MAKING A RETREAT

Fourth Week

A S HAS been told, the "weeks" of the Exercises are of varying lengths. The first two are usually longer than the third; and the last is the shortest. After the spade work of the First Week, which is the purgative stage of the Exercises, the following Two Weeks constitute the illuminative stage. During this period of illumination the soul studies itself and Christ to receive enlightenment about its relationship to Christ. The will can be heroic on occasion, and the occasion is often nothing more than a knowledge of the facts. Certain facts are now presented clearly, which commonly are passed over lightly, if noticed at all, and are half forgotten in a life choked with crowding little interests that reduce life to insignificance and a dull pattern. In the quietude of a Retreat, in the atmosphere, as it were, of eternity, these facts resume their proper dimensions and dispose the will mightily to respond generously to grace. The will, no longer sluggish and somnolent, wakes into life and sensibility. It finds the Third Week a poignant experience.

The Fourth Week, the unitive stage of the Exercises, coming as a blessed relief to feelings bowed down with Christ in His Passion, is not, strange to say, a relaxation of the emotional stress. Different feelings are involved; and, if joy at the good fortune of another can be keener than our compassion with Him in calamity, our feelings in the final Week may be more intense. The comparative brevity of this last stage seems to indicate something of the kind.

The thought sometimes intrudes into meditations on the Passion that Christ knew all along that His short, sharp ordeal would end in resurrection and inconceivable joy, and this knowledge must have tempered His sorrow and pain. And so with our Lady, who understood more fully than the Apostles and followers of Christ the sense of her Son's prophecy that He would rise from the dead. My experience this Week helps me to estimate that thought more accurately. During the Third Week I knew very well what was coming in the Fourth. I did not, as St. Ignatius cautions me, allow my mind to dwell on it; but, of course, I could not exclude it altogether. It was something I knew. I could not not know it. But this knowledge in no way prevented me from being touched by His agony. And, now that the Fourth Week is here, Christ's glory comes, incredible as it may sound, with all the exultant surprise of the unexpected. In one of his general directions for the Week, St. Ignatius bids me to invite a mood of rejoicing at the "great joy and gladness of Christ our Lord," to recall and think about matters likely to cause pleasure, happiness, and joy, such as Heaven, to "avail myself of light, the beauties of the season, as, for example, in summer, of the refreshing coolness; and, in winter, of the sun and of a fire, in proportion as the soul thinks or conjectures that they help it to rejoice in its Creator and Lord." The cheerful mood is usually spontaneous and needs no invitation.

The first contemplation which St. Ignatius sets for the Fourth Week takes us by surprise. In all the meditations and contemplations pertaining to our Lord's life briefly outlined in the Exercises, he confines himself severely to the words of Scripture. In this opening exercise, he asks us to contemplate "How Christ our Lord appeared to our Lady." There is nothing in Scripture about such a meeting. St. Ignatius is so passionately orthodox that we are not prepared to find him taking what seems to be a liberty — even a pious liberty — with the sacred text, and stating as an important fact in connection with our Lord's Resurrection something which none of the Evangelists has recorded. He does not try to justify himself by appealing to tradition. He probably anticipated our surprise, with just a hint of impatience, it seems to me, at our lack of comprehension; for his few words of explanation are short, sharp, and to the point: "He appeared to the Virgin Mary: and, although this is not mentioned in Scripture, still it is considered as mentioned when it says that He appeared to many others, for the Scripture supposes us to have understanding, according as it is written, 'Are ye also without understanding?'"

This curt condescension to unimaginative and meticulous timidity tells us a great deal about St. Ignatius, and is, perhaps, the only instance in the entire Book of Exercises where an intimately personal note is struck. All sayings and incidents on the human side of St. Ignatius have been carefully collected and made the most of by his biographers. They felt that the stern asceticism of his first years after Pampeluna, and the rigorous discipline which, as the founder of a new Religious Order, he imposed upon himself, might leave the erroneous impression that he was a dehumanized and unfeeling leader coldly mathematical in his purposes and heartless in executing them. I do not know that anything has been found which betrays more unmistakably the tenderness under his official manner than this choice of a subject for a most important contemplation in his book. The very curtness of his apology betrays him. He does not know why the sacred writers make no mention of this meeting of Christ and His Blessed Mother. All he knows is that a son will not forget his mother if she is living in his hour of triumph. If she has been made anxious and griefstricken by him in some supreme trial of his manhood, and waits the issue in suspense, the son's first thoughts on coming victorious from the conflict will fly to her, and he will follow them in person as swiftly as he may, with sweet assurance that all is well. That is the way with sons, and that is the way with mothers. If we have any sense at all, we shall not need Revelation to enlighten us on the point. In Christ's own words, "Are ye also without understanding?" Men do not go about telling the world they love their mothers. That is a thing that is taken for granted, so much so that it is ordinarily regarded as a painful breach of good manners to flaunt it in speech.

In contemplating Christ as He appeared to His Blessed Mother and His Apostles and disciples, we are aware of a curious change in our attitude. We associate with Christ, as it were, on a different footing. We are, indeed, still sinners; and death and judgment are still ahead. But, for the time being, these facts have moved back and do not obtrude. Sin and death have been conquered, and we are in the company of the Conqueror. We share some of His security and sense of ease after the fray. Fears and vague apprehensions are for the moment dormant, and love has the soul all to herself. It is a most unusual and exhilarating thing in this probationary world. It is a foretaste of Heaven. "Therefore, if you be risen with Christ, seek the things that are above; where Christ is sitting at the right hand of God: mind the things that are above, not the things that are upon the earth. For you are dead; and your life is hid with Christ in God. When Christ shall appear, who is your life, then you also shall appear with Him in glory."

It is remarkable how vividly the Four Weeks illustrate a passage in Cardinal Newman's "Development" concerning fear and love of God: "Thus we know that no temper of mind is acceptable in the Divine Presence without love; it is love which makes Christian fear differ from servile dread, as true faith differs from the faith of Devils. Yet in the beginning of the religious life, fear is the prominent evangelical grace, and love is but latent in fear, and has in course of time to be developed out of what seems its contradictory. Then, when it is developed, it takes that prominent place which fear held before, yet protecting not superseding it. Love is added, not fear removed, and the mind is but perfected in grace by what seems a revolution. 'They that sow in tears, reap in joy.'"

The fear that was so prominent in the First Week has been gradually receding into the background. During the meditations on Christ's life and Passion, the soul has been coming to be more close and intimate with Him, and so growing in its love of Him that it no longer needs fear to drive it into reluctant fidelities. It is now volunteering for any chance to prove itself. There is no spikenard too rich for lavish outpouring. When love has displaced fear, it is Heaven itself. It is the glorious liberty of sons of God. It is the disposition for ecstatic prayer if that extraordinary grace be not denied.

The crowning exercise of the last Week, toward which the whole Retreat has been moving, is the contemplation for obtaining love. In introducing this exercise, St. Ignatius asks us to keep in mind, while we are making it, two conditions which must be verified in all love that deserves the name, whether human or Divine. The first is "that love ought to show itself in deeds rather than in words." Such was Cordelia's love for her father, "more ponderous than my tongue," not merely heaving "my heart into my mouth." The second condition of all genuine love, St. Ignatius goes on to declare, "consists in mutual interchange on either side, that is to say, in the lover sharing what he has with the beloved, and, on the other hand, in the beloved sharing with the lover, so that, if the one have knowledge, honor, riches, he share it with him who has not, and thus the one share all with the other."

And then we try to recall some of the things God, our Lover, has done for us. We cannot recall more than a few of them, because He gives so stealthily we shall never until eternity know the full measure of His prodigality. Besides, we are in the habit of noting and remembering only those intended blessings which came in the form of trials. We accept the pleasant things as a matter of course. Our grace at meals is often perfunctory: we are likely, if we think about it at all, to think of the host, the cook, the server, the grocer, the milkman, the farmer, rather than of God. If we paid for it, we have one more reason to thank God than the beggar has or the invited guest. After all, He gave us the money to pay for it as He gave everything else.

It is curious how we shuffle and wriggle out of the duty of thanking God. Even men and women who pass as intelligent and accomplished have been known to thank Nature instead of the God of nature, using the capital letter to dignify the mud and metal and rocks out of which the universe is made. What horrible manners, if nothing else, to snap up our morsels and trot off without a glance at the Giver!

The first point is to enumerate the benefits I have received, being conscious always that in the favors which I have received in common with others God had me in mind as clearly and definitely as if I were there exclusively. How thankful I ought to be for my creation, and for my redemption, and for His desire to give me His very self insofar as He can! And can I ever count the particular blessings He has sent me? I must go back to my birth and to long generations before my birth if I am to recall them all. What graciousness was it that led my steps to this holy hour? I can only say, "Take, O Lord, and receive all my liberty, my memory, my understanding, and all my will, all that I have and possess. Thou hast given it to me; to Thee, O Lord, I restore it: all is Thine, dispose of it according to all Thy will. Give me Thy love and Thy grace, for this is enough for me." This is the famous *Suscipe* of St. Ignatius, and it rises spontaneously out of the heart after a review of God's beneficence.

In the second point I consider how God is present in all creation, giving His creatures being, growth, sensation, giving to me all three blessings together with understanding, making of me "a temple, seeing that I am created to the likeness and image of His Divine Majesty." My God is not, indeed, a remote God. And again I say the *Suscipe*.

In the third point, I reflect how God is not only present in all created things in Heaven and on earth, but actually working and laboring in all of them for me. For, not the smallest of them could exist without the inflow of God's sustaining omnipotence. "Take, O Lord, and receive."

In the fourth and last point, I dwell on the thought that all the beauty and loveliness in the world was created by God and is only a faint reflection of His ineffable goodness and beauty. The Greek word for the beautiful is *kalos,* and it is said to come from the Greek word meaning to call. And, indeed, beauty is forever calling us. All beautiful things are the voices of Divine Beauty calling us to Himself. We mangle and kill them when we make them the voices of our own desires. God's sweet, plaintive, patient calling is our vocation to be His children, children of Love and Light and Beauty. This is our true calling. Again say the *Suscipe.*

CHAPTER 6

IGNATIAN SPIRITUALITY:
VOCAL PRAYER

T HE purpose of this chapter is to introduce the subject of a controversy on certain aspects of mystical prayer in connection with the Spiritual Exercises. At present current literature on its more serious side sometimes deals with mysticism as an attractive topic, a strange human experience about which it is more curious than reverential: in this mood, it sometimes finds a book like the Spiritual Exercises too matter of fact and practical. The attitude of literature toward prayer and spirituality is casual and unpredictable; its sudden access of seriousness is likely to be a transitory fashion which could be ignored if it did not seem to find support at times among earnest students of theology and the spiritual life, who here and there and at one time or another have felt impelled to attack the high opinion of the Exercises generally held in the Church. It is to be hoped that a notice of this controversy will contribute to a clearer understanding of the Ignatian system of spirituality.

We must recall some fundamental notions of prayer and solid spirituality which might be lost sight of when inquiry ranges in the higher regions of mystical prayer. The first duty of man is to pray, to worship his Creator, and to have recourse to Him for grace and favors of body and soul. In prayer there is an elevation of the mind and heart to God, communion with Him. The degrees of communion are manifold and supply the grounds for various classifications of prayers. Vocal prayer is the first and most elementary form of prayer; infused contemplation, the highest and last in the progress of divine union. In between, we have mental and discursive prayer, when the mind and memory seek light and understanding, and affective prayer, when the will and imagination and feelings respond to intellectual illumination and attach the soul more closely to God. The prayer of action might also be noted, by which external occupations are turned into prayer by consciously referring them to God and His holy service. This is a very crude outline of a more elaborate diagram which would include many other refinements of division and classification.

None of these various kinds of prayer are wholly exclusive of every other. Vocal prayer is necessarily more or less mental, even if the prayer is in a language we cannot understand, provided, of course, that in it we raise our minds to God. And mental and affective prayer, and even the highest contemplative prayer, need not exclude all verbal expression. Although vocal, mental, and affective prayer are the simpler forms of prayer, and the first to be learned, still they are not simple in another sense. They need some multiplicity of ideas and feelings ordinarily if they are to be sustained for more than the time taken for a swift ejaculatory prayer. The contemplative, on the other hand, needs only a single thought, a single impulse of the heart. He is like a man who is so richly cultivated in an art that he can spend hours gazing in study or rapture upon a single detail in a great picture or famous cathedral where others less accomplished can only keep their interest and attention alive by darting rapidly from one detail to another until they reach the point of exhaustion. For this reason contemplation has been called the prayer of simplification. By cultivating a life of prayer, by long and frequent meditation upon the attributes of God and the beauty of Christ's character, and deepening the understanding of divine truths by trying earnestly to exemplify them experimentally in our conduct, we can, as we advance in perfection and become more sensitive and responsive to divine grace, reach a state where a single word is enough to transport the soul into loving and prolonged communion with God. If these transports are partly the result of our own immediate efforts, after the soul has been, as it were, conditioned by preliminary vocal and mental prayer, the contemplative prayer is what is called acquired contemplation. The very highest kind of prayer is infused contemplation, in which the soul, without effort and without any volition except that of a receptive attitude, is carried beyond the world of the senses and deliberate intellectual processes into some kind of immediate union with God and has experiences akin to, but far short of, the beatific vision of the blessed.

This sublime form of prayer is what is known as mysticism, although the term is often applied less accurately to acquired contemplation. Mystical prayer is a pure gift of God, a most blessed gift, and every lover of God yearns for it as he yearns for the beatific vision in the hereafter. It is the most real example of that foretaste of heaven, which we all dream about hopefully. Yet, it is ordinarily attended, before and after, by trials and sufferings which call for heroic fortitude. It is not a Catholic attitude to depreciate mystical prayer. Neither is it a Catholic attitude to depreciate the lower forms of prayer: this is an error which flourishes principally among those whose interest in prayer is more theoretical than personal and practical. The great mystics are the last people in the world to belittle the need and importance of vocal and discursive prayer in the life of the soul.

In secular literature of the smart contemporary kind, it is not unusual to happen upon passages like the following, which we have culled from a recent publication: "To ask for earthly favors, to reel out a list of requirements and expect them to be supplied is not prayer. It is putting God in the same category as an intelligent grocer." The first comment to be made on this bright sally is that it would be well for all of us if we felt as dependent on God as we do on our grocer. No one can forget about his grocer, while, as a matter of deplorable fact, too many of us too often forget about God. Of course, the reason is that we have not the habit of turning to God in our needs. The grocer, after all, is not the creator of what he supplies us with. He is only one of a series of middle agents which starts where the Creator seems to leave off. The series itself must be upheld by the Creator if it is to get our supplies to us. The passage has a certain air of swaggering pretension which is far from genuinely spiritual. It lacks that simple humility of the child so necessary for the kingdom of God. The filial relationship of the child and its mother is not promoted by discouraging the child from asking because its mother can be trusted in her office of giving.

The literary type of mind is prone to be exacting in its demands of holy persons. It will have the best or nothing. Too often it chooses nothing for itself and leaves the saints to choose the best. The literary conception of what is best is, of course, not always true. The literary man is too often an outsider, the crudest of amateurs, when he begins to discuss religious theory, especially on the subject of prayer. A recent reviewer in the Literary Supplement of the London *Times,* writing about John Wesley, whom he admired greatly, had one serious fault to confess in an otherwise very saintly man. Wesley declared in one of his letters that his first aim was to save his own soul. The reviewer thought it was a low and selfish aim unbecoming a heroic servant of God, who should be wholly absorbed in the interests of God to the utter exclusion of self. It is a curious fact that Henri Bremond and other overenthusiastic writers on mystical prayer fall into the same error, or, at least, seem implicitly to favor it. For error it is, expressly condemned by the Church. Besides the many solemn Scriptural declarations on the primary importance of saving our souls, the lives of mystics like Teresa and Loyola should convince us of the error. To desire union with God, as a mystic does, and not to desire one's own salvation first, is to desire union and not desire it. It is that confusion of mind in which the language of exaggeration so often falls: the false heroics of the special pleader.

Father Henry Bremond approached his treatment of mystical prayer, or pure prayer, from the literary angle. He had written a book on pure poetry, in which he maintained that the experience of the poet in his exalted passages of pure poetry was a natural psychological state similar to that which the mystic experiences in the first stages of pure prayer, or mystical contemplation. His tendency was to ignore or belittle all other kinds of poetry except pure poetry. When we recall that such a shrewd judge of poetry as Gerard Manley Hopkins denied there was a single line of pure poetry in all the poetry of Robert Burns, but at the same time admitted him to the company of great poets as having written the poetry of a vigorous manhood, we can see that Bremond was not keeping his outlook whole. Bremond carries the same tendency — namely, to simplify discussion by the exclusion of unmanageable facts — into his study of mystical prayer. He almost makes one believe that vocal prayer is almost despicable, like uninspired and pedestrian poetry. It is true that poetry suffers if it falls short of being the best. But that cannot be said of prayer, not even vocal prayer. Prayer, no matter how lisping and halting it may be, requires the grace of God. It is a supernatural act with supernatural value far higher than the value of the purest poetry. To regard vocal prayer disdainfully in proclaiming the superior merit of a higher kind of prayer is indulging in the common literary habit of unreal exaggeration.

Certain facts about vocal prayer must be kept in mind to preserve a right scale of values. In the first place, as has been said, it is a supernatural act needing divine impulse and inspiration. When our Lord was asked by His Apostles to teach them how to pray, He taught them the "Our Father." Moreover, He promised His divine presence in a special way to those who came together in His name for prayer in common. He Himself used vocal prayer in the most solemn moments of His life on earth. His Church makes the recitation of vocal prayers a condition for the gaining of indulgences. The canon reads:

"If prayer for the Pope's intentions is prescribed for gaining indulgences, mental prayer alone does not suffice; the faithful may say whatever vocal prayer they wish unless some special prayer is prescribed." The Mass, the divine office, the entire liturgy, bear witness to the importance attached by the Church to set vocal prayers.

Another fact to be remembered to keep our ideas clear is that vocal prayer is not an elementary form suited only to beginners in the spiritual life. It was cultivated and practised throughout their lives by all the saints no matter to what mystical heights they were called. Cardinal Newman, who, as far as human judgment can see, was the greatest spiritual force in English-speaking countries during the nineteenth century, is quoted by a member of his religious community as having declared that he prayed best with a pen in his hand. Only an extremely literal-minded person would deny that the writing of one's prayer was vocal, as well as mental, prayer.

CHAPTER 7

SCHOOLS OF SPIRITUALITY

THE literature of the spiritual life has been divided into various groups or schools of writers. Thus we have the Benedictine School, the Dominican, the Franciscan, the Carmelite, the Redemptorist, the Jesuit, the School of St. Francis of Sales, the French School of the seventeenth century, associated with the name of Cardinal de Berulle, who founded the Oratorians in France. Any reader who desires to go into the subject can find information in Pourrat's *Christian Spirituality,* which is exhaustive, and in Tanquerey's very excellent *Spiritual Life.*

What is called Jesuit spirituality is not in essentials at all different from that of other Catholic schools. Union with God in prayerful habits, or what is called a life of perfection, is the object of all Catholic spirituality in and out of religious houses. Jesuits do not attach less value to acquired or to infused contemplation than do Carmelites or Benedictines; and the latter do not depreciate the laborious acquisition of virtue or zeal in God's service. Jesuits find good spiritual reading in every school; and Jesuit works are popular in other religious families. Father Bouscaren, a Jesuit of whom more will be seen in a succeeding chapter, numbered among his favorite authors Cardinal Manning and the Benedictine Abbot Marmion. St. Thomas Aquinas, St. Alphonsus Liguori, St. Teresa, St. John of the Cross, St. Francis of Sales; these, to mention a few, and their disciples, are, needless to say, standard authors among Jesuits.

Hence, when we speak of schools of spirituality it would be a grave mistake to suppose that, in the broader aspect of the spiritual life and in most of its details, there was any hard and fast division. A Jesuit has something to learn in all of them for his own profit. In the time of St. Ignatius, there were no so-called schools of spirituality: the classification into schools arose in the seventeenth century from the French passion for precision. St. Ignatius found spiritual sustenance wherever he could; and so still do his sons. The affective prayer and liturgical piety of the Benedictines, the contemplative vocation of the Carmelites, the humble simplicity of the Franciscans, the Thomistic reverence and apostolic spirit of the Dominicans, the special devotional aptitudes and practices of all religious families in the Church, have nothing rigidly exclusive about them as fuel for spiritual ardor. The language of the soul is the same whether coming from St. Augustine, the Curé of Ars, St. Thomas More, or the Little Flower: among the close friends of Christ, there are no distinctions of vernacular and dialect, no caste, no manneristic idioms.

The grounds for any classification into schools is the particular emphasis placed upon one or another aspect of perfection, one or another way of advancing in it. All of these different aspects and methods have official approval, and are so many facets of the same wonderful thing: the soul's yearning for union with its divine Lover. Their diversity does not modify essentials while it serves the purpose of suiting and satisfying the variety of needs to be found in a world where natural temperaments, dispositions, and qualities of mind and body are so various.

Most readers of spiritual literature never think of asking to what school of spirituality a book belongs. Indeed, the school is not always easy to determine unless the book is frankly controversial. It is not uncommon to see a work assigned to different schools according to the preferences of the critics. A Jesuit reader of Father de Caussade's classic, *L'Abandon,* sees in it an amplification and development of two leading points in the Spiritual Exercises of St. Ignatius. This is so obvious to him as not to need the confirmation which the late Dom Chapman, Abbot of Downside, gives in his introduction to another of Father de Caussade's works translated into English under the title, *On Prayer*. The Benedictine Abbot tells us that Father de Caussade in his *L'Abandon* derived his doctrine from St. Ignatius, "who begins and ends his Exercises with this simple and sublime teaching: in the Foundation he lays it down dryly with irresistible logic; in the final *Contemplatio ad Amorem*, he spiritualizes it as the conclusion of the whole retreat: *Sume et suscipe, Domine, universam meam libertatem*. I hope the reader knows this prayer by heart. It is very dear to every son of St. Ignatius; it sums up religion and perfection: it is exactly what Père de Caussade reiterates in every key."

After this firm expression of coincidence with the Jesuit view on the part of the Abbot, who was an authority on the subject, there would seem to be no room for discussion; or, at least, if the matter were debatable, the claims of the Exercises as a possible influence in *L'Abandon* would seem to demand consideration. Now comes a curious instance of what I meant when I said it is not always easy to place the correct school label on a spiritual book. Two years after Abbot Chapman's introduction appeared, Father de Caussade's *L'Abandon* was published in English dress with the title, *Self-abandonment to Divine Providence*, with an introduction by another Benedictine monk of the same Abbey. In this introduction the writer says: "Père de Caussade's spiritual teaching was derived from two extremely pure sources, St. Francis of Sales and St. John of the Cross." He also mentions Bossuet. He makes no reference whatever to St. Ignatius or his Exercises.

The ascription of spiritual writers to particular schools is a matter of little or no importance: their ordinary purpose is to edify, not to exploit a school; and the general run of readers look to them for inspiration and instruction and not for curious erudition about derivations. All schools of spirituality must derive from the teachings of Christ and His Church; these are the only sources with which the reader of a spiritual book need be concerned. The saints were not concerned with so-called schools. "St. Philip," says Newman, "on one occasion, acknowledged his debt in one particular to the elder saint: he said to some Jesuits whom he met, 'You are the children of a great Father. I am under obligations to him; for your Master, Ignatius, taught me to make mental prayer.'"

CHAPTER 8

ABBÉ HENRI BREMOND

A T THE turn of the century in France the subject of mystical prayer was beginning to be a favorite subject with Catholic writers on the spiritual life. A controversy developed as to whether mystical contemplation was for all or only for a few who were divinely called to that high prayer. Out of this controversy in the succeeding decades of the century arose the attack on the Spiritual Exercises and Jesuit spirituality. The Exercises, which Melchior Cano, a famous Dominican theologian of the sixteenth century, had violently accused of being too mystical, were now criticized for not being mystical at all and for discouraging aspiration to mystical contemplation. The foremost champion in this new controversy and the one who, by his writing gift and brilliant attainments, turned the floodlight on it, was the Abbé Henri Bremond, an ex-Jesuit. He was another Pascal putting genius at the service of less articulate critics and giving them the advantage of eloquence and skill in public debate.

Henri Bremond entered the Society in 1882 at the age of eighteen and distinguished himself in his studies, especially on the humanistic side. He was attached to the editorial staff of *Études,* the French Jesuit monthly, from 1899 to 1904, the year he left the Society. His severance from the Society arose out of the modernist movement which he skirted cautiously while having some sympathy with its leaders. One of them, the excommunicated Father George Tyrrell, was an old and much admired friend; and, when he was dying in 1907, Bremond braved ecclesiastical censure to be at his bedside and incurred the usual penalty of suspension for a brief space. For the rest, Father Bremond remained in good standing among the French clergy until his death in 1933.

Bremond was a voluminous writer. His favorite subjects were religion and sanctity, treated from a humanistic point of view, which imparted absorbing interest to subjects usually approached by only the most serious readers. The wide literary appeal of his books must have been a strong influence in the Catholic revival among French men of letters. The first volume of his great *Literary History of Religious Sentiment in France* appeared in 1915. It was dedicated to "Devout Humanism." The eleventh and last volume was published in 1933 when the author was dying, with his *opus magnum* unfinished. In 1923 he had been elected a member of the French Academy.

Some of Bremond's books have been translated and published in English. One of them, *Prayer and Poetry,* gives an excellent idea of his method. The theory which he advocates in it is, as has been mentioned in a preceding chapter, that pure poetry and pure prayer — that is, mystical prayer — are identical experiences up to a certain point. His thesis is hardly anything more than an interesting conjecture. But, before the author finishes, the reader is ready to accept it as a demonstrated proposition. It is wonderful what an array of witnesses Bremond brings forward in support of his contention. He ransacks all known literatures, ancient and modern, and adduces confirmatory passages from the writings of philosophers, poets, saints, unbelievers, mundane authors, and authorities on Catholic mysticism. The quotations are carefully selected from their contexts and are so numerous as to be convincing, as well as delectable, to the lover of curious literature.

It can hardly be denied that there is much truth in the observation of the French Jesuit, Father de Guibert, that the *History of Religious Sentiment* is not properly a history but rather a series of essays. Bremond was an essayist and not an historian. Like Lord Macaulay, he simply had to be brilliant and he played up the features of his subject which allowed his special talents to shine. It is not a continuous and objective narrative, in which perspective and proportion are preserved, but a collection of monographs in which the author was led by his own preferences and in which, to employ his own word, he "orchestrated" beautiful and striking passages from neglected writers to drive his point home and to startle the literary world into a revision of its concepts of religious writers.

There is no objection to a humanistic treatment of religious themes. It may be considered desirable and even necessary on the principle that, if the truth is to be preached and understood, it must be conveyed in language which the hearers know. But to preach the Catholic religion to a world in its best literary medium is a more perilous enterprise than preaching it in a Chinese dialect. Newman could do it without losing his head and being betrayed into the errors he was opposing. Bremond, who had great admiration for Newman, had not Newman's strong grasp of truth nor his seriousness of purpose. Newman would have allowed himself to be drawn and quartered before he would consciously write about his own or anyone else's religious experiences for literary effect. He once declared that he had never written anything for a purely literary purpose. There is no wish to accuse Bremond flatly of being primarily literary in his discussions of religion. But he lacks the tremendous seriousness of Newman so obviously that the suspicion is unavoidable. At least on one occasion he overstepped the bounds in his *Life of St. Jane Frances de Chantal,* which was placed on the Index in 1913, shortly after its publication. And can anyone imagine Cardinal Newman writing *The Thundering Abbot* (*l'abbé Tempête*), in which the great reformer, Armand de Rancé, was unjustly put on exhibition for the amusement of polite drawing rooms?

No, Bremond was not another Newman. The great Cardinal did not write for literary circles. Nor did he play with ideas. In Bremond's "Poetry and Prayer," the author is so entranced

with his theory that he creates the impression that there is no
great poetry outside of pure poetry; and this is not true. Still
more untrue is the impression left with the reader that there
is no worthy prayer short of contemplative prayer. While we all
agree that mediocrity in poetry may have little or no excuse
for existence, prayer, as a supernatural act, must be judged by
altogether different standards. Halting verses are inexcusable,
but halting prayers have a value transcending the value of the
purest poetry. Abbé Bremond, of course, knew this very well,
and he introduces a footnote to save himself. But the tenor of
the footnote and the drift of the text are in opposite directions.

In view of Bremond's admiration for Cardinal Newman, it
is interesting to recall what the latter says of the book which
receives his adverse criticism. In the eleventh chapter of the
Development of Christian Doctrine, Newman says: "St. Ignatius's Spiritual Exercises are among the most approved methods
of devotion in the modern Catholic Church; they proceed from
one of the most celebrated of her Saints, and have the praise of
Popes, and of the most eminent masters of the spiritual life. A
Bull of Paul the Third's 'approves, praises, and sanctions all and
everything contained in them'; indulgences are granted to the
performance of them by the same Pope, by Alexander the
Seventh, and by Benedict the Fourteenth. St. Carlo Borromeo
declared that he had learned more from them than from all
other books together; St. Francis de Sales calls them 'a holy
method of reformation,' and they are the model on which all
the extraordinary devotions of religious men or bodies, and the
course of missions, are conducted. If there is a document which
is the authoritative exponent of the inward communion of the
members of the modern Catholic Church with their God and
Saviour, it is this work." Twenty years later, in the "Apologia,"
writing about his Anglican days, Newman tells us the impression made on him by the Exercises in a passage which is quoted
in the appendix.

It is nearly a hundred years ago since Newman wrote that

the Exercises had the praise of Popes and were among the most approved methods of devotion in the modern Catholic Church. Another chapter will itemize the principal objections urged against the Exercises by Bremond and his fellow critics. Have these objections, during the past thirty years or more, affected the high standing of the Exercises in the official mind of the Church? It is a natural query, which can be answered at once.

The late Pope, His Holiness Pius XI, published an Encyclical Letter, *Mens Nostra,* urging the wider use of spiritual exercises among clergy and laity and recommending above all other methods that of St. Ignatius. The Encyclical appeared December 20, 1929, and it is not unnatural to see in it an implicit judgment in the controversy on the Exercises then waging in France. The following passages from the Letter are a striking confirmation of everything Newman claimed for the place held by the Exercises in the modern Church:

"Now it is recognized that among all the methods of spiritual exercises which very laudably adhere to the principle of sound Catholic asceticism, one has ever held the foremost place and, adorned by the full and repeated approbation of the Holy See and honored by the praises of men distinguished for spiritual doctrine and sanctity, has borne abundant fruits of holiness during the space of well nigh four hundred years. We mean the method introduced by St. Ignatius of Loyola, whom We are pleased to call the chief and peculiar Master of Spiritual Exercises. His 'admirable book of Exercises,' ever since it was solemnly approved, praised, and commended by Our Predecessor Paul III of happy memory, already (to repeat some words We once used before Our elevation to the Chair of Peter) already, We say, 'stood forth conspicuous as a most wise and universal code of laws for the direction of souls in the way of salvation and perfection; as a perennial fountain of most excellent and most solid piety; as a most keen stimulus, and a competent guide on the way to secure amendment of morals and to attain the summit of the spiritual life.'

"When at the beginning of Our Pontificate, 'satisfying the most ardent desires and wishes of sacred Prelates of both Rites throughout almost the whole Catholic world' in the Apostolic Constitution *Summorum Pontificum,* given on July 25, 1922, We 'declared and constituted St. Ignatius of Loyola the heavenly Patron of all spiritual exercises, and, therefore, of institutes, sodalities, and bodies of every kind assisting those who are making spiritual exercises,' We did little else but sanction by Our supreme authority what was already proclaimed by the common feeling of Pastors and the Faithful; and what together with the aforesaid Paul III, Our illustrious Predecessors, Alexander VII, Benedict XIV, Leo XIII, had often said implicitly when praising the Ignatian meditations, and what all those who, in the words of Leo XIII, 'had been conspicuous for ascetic doctrine or holiness of life' during the last four hundred years had said by their praises and still more by the example they gave of the virtues which they had acquired in these exercises.

"Indeed, the excellence of the spiritual doctrine entirely free from the perils and errors of false mysticism, the admirable adaptability of the Exercises to any order or state of men, whether they devote themselves to contemplation in the cloister or lead an active life in the affairs of the world, the apt co-ordination of the various parts, the wonderful and lucid order in the meditation on truths that seem to follow naturally one from another; and lastly the spiritual lessons which, after casting off the yoke of sin and washing away the diseases inherent in his conduct, lead a man through the safe paths of abnegation and the removal of evil habits up to the supreme heights of prayer and Divine love—all this is enough to show beyond a doubt the efficacious nature of the Ignatian method and is preponderating evidence in favor of the Ignatian meditations."

In these words Pius XI unmistakably denies the validity of criticism which asserts that the Ignatian method is too rigid and formal and hampers the movements of the soul in prayer, that it is not co-ordinated, that it discourages when it does not ignore mystical contemplation, that it has ceased to be what its founder intended it to be.

In further confirmation of Newman's statement that, "if there is a document which is the authoritative exponent of the inward communion of the members of the modern Catholic Church with their God and Saviour, it is this book," namely, the book of Spiritual Exercises of St. Ignatius, attention is drawn to a decree of the Sacred Congregation on the Sacraments, dated April 27, 1928. The decree concerned a difficulty submitted to the Congregation on the canonical law requiring the candidate for Holy Orders to make the Spiritual Exercises before ordination. In a note to the decree, the Secretary of the Congregation expressly declares that the exercises signified in the canon are "the Spiritual Exercises of St. Ignatius of Loyola, the Founder of the Society of Jesus." He declares further that St. Charles Borromeo, and later St. Vincent de Paul, had enforced this provision of making the Spiritual Exercises as a strict rule for all their candidates to the priesthood, concluding with the words: "and this rule of St. Vincent de Paul was in force throughout the Church either through particular law, or custom, up to the time of the promulgation of the Code."

Pius XI's esteem was shared, as he says, by his great predecessor, Leo XIII. In an Apostolic Letter on the Exercises, addressed to the General of the Society in February, 1900, he testified to the peculiar power of the Exercises in promoting the welfare of individuals and commonwealths. And addressing the clergy of Carpineto, he said: "I have striven in many ways to be of service to my birthplace; but nothing I have done has, I think, proved a greater boon to it and a greater comfort to myself than to have made it possible for the clergy there to follow the Spiritual Exercises. What I can never forget is, that, while my whole soul was eagerly yearning for a more substantial food, I sought for it in vain in many books; not one satisfied me until I came upon St. Ignatius's Book of the Spirtual Exercises.

Keenly did I relish it, and bethought me: Here is what my soul was craving for. Nor have I ever parted with it since. The Meditation on the End of Man alone would suffice to consolidate anew the whole social fabric."

CHAPTER 9

BREMOND'S CRITICISM

THE long tradition of high favor in which the Spiritual Exercises have been held by popes, bishops, secular and regular clergy, by canonized saints and religious-minded men and women, is the most effective answer to the criticism directed against the Exercises and the type of spirituality which they promote. That criticism, as has been indicated, comes for the most part from a literary revival of interest in mysticism. But it comes, too, from serious and devout writers, comparatively few, who sincerely advocate the adoption of mystical modes of prayer as particularly suited to the modern type of mind and disposition. It is a type that is nervous, impatient of routine, method, and systematic discipline, unequal to the demands of asceticism, rebellious against tradition, and yet not without generous impulses and a craving for religious truth and experience. We are familiar with the type. We are not so sure that it is an exclusively modern product; but perhaps it is more prevalent just now. However, indulgence of this humor to make it holy by stimulating it emotionally with the prospects of a mysterious experience, which is usually the final stage of an intensely ascetical progress, seems unwise and not in complete accord with the teaching of Christ and the Church. Self-abnegation is the law of spiritual advancement declared by Christ and heroically put into practice by the saints. One cannot get around it. To relegate it to the background and interpret it liberally is building without a foundation. The modern mind may not like the law of self-abnegation but there it is, nevertheless.

Father Bremond's quarrel with Ignatian spirituality is principally that it is ascetical and revolves around self instead of around God. It is taken up too much with examinations of conscience, mechanical devices for insuring success, vigilance over self, penitential practices to acquire virtue and overcome faults, formal methods, constant checking of procedure. Father Bremond invented a label for his conception of Ignatian prayer which has the merit of summing up his whole argument in one condemnatory word. He calls it anthropocentric; and he contrasts it with what he calls theocentric prayer, in which the soul is more concerned with God and union with Him than with itself. One other brilliantly coined label was employed to discredit and cast suspicion upon Ignatian prayer: panhedonistic prayer, a form of anthropocentric, in which the soul is thinking more of its own peace and consolation than of the glory and the love of God.

These are masterly generalizations with enough stiffening of obvious facts to make them stand until they are coldly scrutinized and challenged. There is no doubt whatever that pure theocentric prayer is absolutely the very best. It is the kind of prayer we shall all use in heaven, where the soul has been confirmed in perfection and need watch itself no longer nor have to strive laboriously to fix its mind on God, and where it enjoys forever the peace and consolation of God's sweet Presence. But, alas, we are not in heaven yet. We are still on probation, on the testing field, being subjected to trials of mettle and endurance, with certain little inherited or acquired flaws in our mechanism that need watching. A sane realism suggests that prayer in these circumstances must be somewhat anthropocentric.

If prayer were wholly anthropocentric, it would be mere superstition and would be condemned by the Church; as, on the other hand, a prayer that is too mystical for this world has been condemned. Miguel de Molinos, the founder of Quietism, was condemned in the seventeenth century for teaching the doctrine that, if we practised interior annihilation and contemplative prayer, we might commit any carnal sins without incurring guilt: the sins were from the devil and not from us. Virtue still stands in the middle; and the Church is there to see that it does.

Is Ignatian prayer too anthropocentric? The foundation principle, the basic proposition, on which the whole Spiritual Exercises rests, is the primary truth about the purpose of our existence. St. Ignatius, as is generally known, put it this way: Man was created to praise, reverence, and serve God our Lord, and by this means to save his soul. The giving of glory can be defined as the giving of praise, reverence, and service, so that the phrase can be shortened: "Man was created to give glory to God and by this means to save his soul." Can this statement of our end and purpose be characterized as anthropocentric? It gives the keynote to Ignatian spirituality. The glory of God was uppermost in the mind of St. Ignatius. It is continually coming up in the Exercises and made the point of reference in arriving at decisions and formulating plans of life. The idea of God's glory is the ruling idea of the Constitutions of the Society of Jesus; the motto of the Society, *Ad Majorem Dei Gloriam* — For the Greater Glory of God — is associated so commonly with the Society of Jesus that the initials, A.M.D.G., are almost a trade-mark.

Does a man's solicitude to save his soul make his prayer and spiritual life so anthropocentric as to be sinful? or even less perfect? God wants us to save our soul, and He gives us graces, and arranges the conditions and circumstances of our life, solely that we may be able to work out that divine purpose. *That* glory He requires, and it coincides with our perfection and eternal happiness. Is it, then, to be seriously regarded as a sign of high perfection to be concerned with the glory of God in everything except in the matter of saving our soul? Father Bremond seems to think so. To say equivalently, "I will love God so much that I shall not care whether I lose my soul or not" indicates a kind of mental confusion not characteristic of the saints.

Is it the selfishness of a small, mean, narrow soul to be always concerned about its salvation? Here, I think, is where discussion sometimes tends to go astray. A little reflection should show that no man thinks so seldom about himself, in the selfish sense of the word, as the man who has an earnest desire to save his soul, and directs all his efforts to that end. He has to think of God always. When he thinks of himself, it is only to measure his performance with what God expects of him. His eyes are on God; his ears are tuned in on the Voice of God, and tuned out on all other voices, most of all on the voice of self; His hands and feet are quick to obey, his speech jealously controlled by, the thought of God. If everybody in the world were eagerly intent on saving his soul, what a lovely world it would be! It would be a world so devoid of selfishness as to be difficult to picture. Divine truth has many paradoxes, hard to be understood by an unspiritual world, and one of them is this: the more selfish we are in the interests of our soul, the less selfish we shall be.

To enter into a detailed discussion of Bremond's criticism of Ignatian spirituality as anthropocentric and panhedonistic does not enter into the scope of this book. According to the principles of that criticism, all the liturgical prayers of the Church would have to be regarded with something like disdain as the expressions of an inferior kind of spirituality. In the Exercises and in the Constitutions of his Society, St. Ignatius is always and most of all careful to ascertain the mind of the Church and to conform to it as to a norm of divine wisdom. Thinking with the Church is the first rule he lays down for all followers of Christ, and, of course, for his Society. If the Exercises are not more anthropocentric or panhedonistic than the liturgy of the Church or the practice of the faithful, in every plane of holiness and perfection, throughout the ages, they may be regarded as a fairly safe guide in the spiritual life, up to and including mystical heights. The mind of the Church, as expressed in papal and episcopal documents, undoubtedly holds them in esteem, and certainly does not hold them to be antimystical.

To explain how it came to be that St. Ignatius, who was a mystic, could favor an antimystical school of spirituality, Bremond introduced a novel historical explanation. The book of the Spiritual Exercises, according to this explanation, while sinning on the side of asceticism and logical coherence, was not altogether antimystical. But in practical use, the intention of its author was perverted by the *Directorium,* an official commentary on the Exercises, got out in 1599 under the direction of the General of the Society, Father Acquaviva, for the instruction and guidance of Jesuits giving retreats. The purpose of the commentary, according to Father Bremond, was to rescue the book of Spiritual Exercises, which had been experiencing an "eclipse" since the death of St. Ignatius. The directions here given retreat masters, to make the Exercises more popular, departed substantially from the original purpose of their saintly author.

What are the facts?

1. The approval of the Exercises by popes, bishops, and saints for three centuries, we may suppose, made no nice distinction between the book of Exercises and its actual use in retreats. It is more probable that these high authorities had in mind the retreats and their fruits rather than the book itself.

2. During the eclipse, which the book of Spiritual Exercises is said to have suffered, thirteen editions of it appeared. For a small book, wholly lacking in style to ease its severe demands on a reader's attention, this is not a bad record. It is one of the most famous books in the world, but one may well doubt whether in any succeeding period of fifty years thirteen editions have been called for. Moreover, the book was printed for private circulation, since it was regarded as of little use to anyone without a director, and might be harmful.

3. The preface of the *Directorium* informs us that tentative copies of it had been printed and put into circulation for some years, *aliquot annos,* among Jesuits for the purpose of gathering

the best opinions in the Society and embodying them in a final and permanent form. These opinions were discussed and sifted by a general congregation of the whole Society before the *Directorium* finally took shape. It was no one man's work. It was the considered and concerted commentary of the whole Society on a book of its founder, which was the basis of its spiritual life.

4. Considering five years as a conservative estimate of the length of time during which the *Directorium* was undergoing the process of critical scrutiny and revision, we may set 1594 as the date when the proposal of a *Directorium* was launched in its tentative form. That would be thirty-eight years after the death of St. Ignatius. Many of the Saint's contemporaries were still alive. Some of them, like St. Peter Canisius, who died in 1597, had been trained in the spiritual life by the holy founder. St. Robert Bellarmine, Suarez, Lessius were some among the older generation of Jesuits to whom the *Directorium* was submitted for examination. To suppose that they consented without protest to an interpretation of the text of the Spiritual Exercises which went counter to the intention of its author exceeds the bounds of historical credibility.

5. The book of Spiritual Exercises and the *Directorium* are both easily accessible for anyone who cares to verify Father Bremond's discovery in the field of history.

Much is made of an apparent disinclination of the Society to encourage mystical contemplation. If my testimony on this point is worth declaring, I wish to say that during fifty years in the Society I have never seen or heard or read in the life or in the rules or in the exhortations of superiors anything which might be construed as the setting of a limit to progress in prayer. If a Jesuit is faithful to his rules, there is no doubt whatever that he will arrive at that condition of the soul where the grace of mystical prayer may be bestowed. It is a purely gratuitous favor of God and may be withheld in the best conditions. It is not in itself the surest index of perfection in a heroic degree. The only sure index is that given by Christ and consists in doing the will of God, with or without gracious visitations in prayer. The Constitutions of the Society and the Spiritual Exercises concentrate on conformity with the will of God in all things; and a virtuous life is considered a more infallible sign of perfection than mystical experiences. The latter can be, and often have been, false and illusory, coming not from God but from the spirit of darkness or from a fevered mind too intent upon the heights to be scrupulously concerned with the painful approaches. It would be more pleasant for everyone to skip the ascetical preparation for mystical favors; and, as human nature is constituted, there is constant temptation to make short cuts to the peaks. If the Society lays emphasis on the laborious stages, and leaves the rest to the operations of the Holy Spirit, it would seem to be following the only prudent course. It is a course that has not prevented Jesuits from becoming saints and arriving, like their father, Ignatius, at the enjoyment of mystical experiences.

It is true the Society is not a contemplative Order and does not make contemplative prayer its primary end. Its end is to enter the arena of the world and labor for souls, cultivating at the same time habits of prayer and aiming at personal perfection on Ignatian lines. Its form of religious life has been called "mixed" because it is both active and contemplative. Father Anthony Huonder, S.J., describes the attitude of St. Ignatius toward the purely contemplative life as follows: "The ideal of virtue and of prayer in the Society was determined by the apostolic spirit. Hence to abandon or neglect the care of souls for love of solitude and contemplation was absolutely contrary to the spirit of the Order; and the opinion that the glory of God was better promoted by contemplation was opposed by the Saint. This he explained by a comparison. A king had two sons: one he dispatched on certain important business involving the conduct of a difficult war; the other son he kept at home for companionship. In which of the two did he repose the greater confidence and which had the greater opportunity of earning his gratitude and experiencing his bounty? This comparison applies to those who sacrifice contemplation to dedicate themselves to works of charity and arduous undertakings."

The view here expressed does not differ from that of the great contemplative, St. Theresa of Jesus (*Works,* V; Exclamations II, p. 324). "How great is the love You bear the children of men: the worthiest service we can give You is to leave You for love of them and for their greater good."

They are two different vocations: that to the life of the Society and that to a purely contemplative life. If in the history of the Society there are instances of official rebuke administered for the practice or encouragement of mystical contemplation, they can be explained in every case by one of two facts. The recipient of the rebuke was either departing materially from his vocation by neglect of his duty, in the cultivation of mystical favors; or he was laying excessive value on mystical experiences as a sole criterion of holiness and perfection, and encouraging forced and premature efforts among beginners in the spiritual life with the usual results of fantasy, self-complacence, and delusion.

No list of authorities on mystical contemplation would be complete without the names of a score of Jesuits whose works on the subject were published with the approval of their superiors. These books not only praise that form of prayer as the very highest but instruct and encourage readers to hope for it. That great classic, *Practice of Christian Perfection,* by Alphonsus Rodriguez, a much-used textbook for three hundred years inside and outside of the Society, has been accused of sowing suspicion of mystical prayer and deprecating efforts to attain it. The accusation is unjust and rests on passages in which Father Rodriguez is careful to warn beginners against the peril of setting out too wide a spread of sail for the size of their boat. Anyone who looks for it can easily find in the book ample recognition of mystical prayer as the highest form of divine union in prayer. In an Apostolic Letter to the Superiors of Religious Orders, March 29, 1924, Pius XI recommends Rodriguez with St. Bernard and Bonaventure as a spiritual writer: "The strength and efficacy of his writings far from diminishing with the years, seem today to be better than ever."

It is doubtful whether a psychologist will find fault with the caution exercised by the Society in those mysterious borders where aberrations of mind and heart wait indiscretion at every turn. Prayer, vocal and mental, self-discipline, and the practice of virtue are the duties at our door; the rest can be left to the Holy Spirit. Whether Tabor be an extraordinary experience of the devout soul or the normal and ordinary culmination of a life of fidelity to grace, need not be discussed. In any case they are more likely to find it who are too humble to expect it. Its indiscriminate exploitation, as in the seventeenth century, can be productive of a large crop of vagaries, extravagances, and heresies.

In this connection, Ignatian spirituality has been charged with a pelagian tendency to depend too much on personal effort and too little on the grace of God. While it is supremely true that we cannot take a step toward our salvation without the grace of God, it is still true that we must cooperate with grace. It is just as much a heresy to say that the grace of God will save us irrespective of our works as to say our works will save us without the need of grace. Against this twofold heresy, so prominent in his times, St. Ignatius laid down a boldly worded principle of action: "This is the first rule to be observed in every undertaking: Trust God as if its success depended entirely on you and in no whit on God; but at the same time bend all your energies to the business in hand as if you were doing nothing at all and God were doing everything." As one might infer from the official approval, long continued and strongly expressed, the Spiritual Exercises do not contain a single passage capable of a pelagian interpretation.

The criticism, that the Exercises overstress the intellectual preparation for affective prayer to the detriment of spiritual freedom, is discussed fully and clearly by Professor Alfred O'Rahilly in his *Father William Doyle, S.J., A Spiritual Study*. The reader is referred to that part of his book entitled "Jesuit Prayer" for a more detailed and far better treatment of the subject than anything I can give within the limits I have set myself.

In conclusion, I wish to call attention to the fact that the Society of Jesus has been especially entrusted with the work of promoting the devotion to the Sacred Heart. This devotion has for its object the cultivation and increase of love of God in the soul. It is a devotion which inspires and encourages affective prayer and it has been the favorite devotion of the Society for nearly three centuries.

CHAPTER 10

PIUS XI AND THE EXERCISES

THE encyclical, from which I have quoted in the preceding chapter, was not a mere official gesture conforming
with a long papal tradition. It carried with it a strong personal
note. It expressed convictions formed and tried by years of
actual experience in making and giving the Exercises. For
thirty years the future Pius XI was not only a distinguished
Doctor of the Ambrosian Library; he was at the same time
the chaplain of the Cenacle convent in Milan. The record of
those thirty years as chaplain is impressive. Besides the ordinary duties of a chaplain, daily Mass, Benediction, instructions
to the community, there were weekly classes in Christian doctrine, apologetics, and monthly retreats to various classes of
women. Children were prepared for First Communion and
there was a sermon every day during the months of May and
June. In the congenial labors of the famous Library Father
Achille Ratti's spiritual interests and apostolic zeal were not
allowed to grow dormant.

Father Philip Hughes, the archivist of Westminster Cathedral, London, and the biographer of the late Pope, in an article
appearing in the *Dublin Review* after the death of Pius XI,
comments as follows on those thirty years of chaplaincy:

"What the spirit was that directed the preacher through all
these years, and, directing him, formed him, everyone can
divine, once everyone knows that these nuns of the Cenacle
not only follow a rule constructed for them by the Jesuits
after the pattern of the rule of the Society, but were founded
for the purpose of themselves giving retreats according to the

system of St. Ignatius. The whole *raison d'être* of the Cenacle nun, in the intentions of those who founded the Institute, was to teach souls to pray, and to regulate their lives, along the lines of the Spiritual Exercises. What, to the best of his power, and with a continual study of the instrument he used, Pius XI was doing all these years at the Cenacle was what is the fundamental occupation of every Jesuit the world over, the regulation of his own life and the direction of others in the spirit of the Spiritual Exercises of St. Ignatius. To the Pope's understanding of this spirit there are many testimonies. There is the monograph, written while in the Cenacle, in which he sets forth his own discovery that St. Charles Borromeo, instituting the custom of clergy retreats, and building a house where they could be given, had these retreats ordered on the lines of the Spiritual Exercises. There are, later, the several papal letters, such, for example, as the famous *Meditantibus Nobis* to the Jesuit General on the occasion of the third centenary of the canonization of St. Ignatius, and the encyclical on retreats, *Mens Nostra,* where the spiritual method of St. Ignatius is given a singularly definite preference over all others, and the Saint is made the patron of the whole work of retreats throughout the Church."

In reviewing the career of Pius XI, Father Hughes does not hesitate to declare that in his chaplaincy in Milan, to which he was appointed at the age of twenty-five, the late pope met "the third of the great forces that shaped his character, something greater than anything he had hitherto encountered. He met the very spirit of Ignatius Loyola, and his humanist, renaissance intelligence, and indeed his whole soul, *anima naturaliter Ignatiana,* leapt to the embrace."

In the course of his article, Father Hughes makes no reference to the Apostolic Letter which Pius XI sent to Cardinal Dubois, Archbishop of Paris, on the occasion of a program of spiritual revival instituted by the Cardinal in his diocese during Easter week of 1929. The seventh and eighth volumes of the *History of Religious Sentiment,* the volumes in which Bremond criticized the Jesuit method of prayer, had appeared some months before and were everywhere the subject of lively discussion. It is impossible to avoid the belief that this letter was intended to counteract the effects of Bremond's criticism and to reassure minds that might be bewildered and dazzled by its brilliant rhetoric and masterful manipulation of history.

The only way this letter to Cardinal Dubois differs from the encyclical, *Mens Nostra,* issued later in the year to the whole Church is the more personal note to be observed in it. "We are happy," the letter runs, "to testify once again to the zeal and piety which prompt you to promote whatever can contribute to the spiritual progress and sanctification of clergy and laity. It gives Us keen pleasure to see you securing the precious fruits of a retreat by recommending the method of St. Ignatius. It is a method which Our Predecessors, from the time of Paul III, have recommended, and which has been practised with relish by so many Saints for the sanctification of their souls and the welfare of the faithful in every walk of life.

"Indeed, the Exercises of St. Ignatius have a peculiar power of elevating souls and leading them to the summits of Prayer and Divine Love along the sure paths of abnegation and mastery over our passions. And they do this without exposing the soul to the subtle illusions of pride.

"We Ourselves in the course of the sacred ministry have had the opportunity of testing by experience the salutary effectiveness of the Spiritual Exercises of St. Ignatius, and We can testify to the advancement in perfection realized by souls in following these Exercises.

"We bless, then, with a special earnestness, all those who will participate in the Week of retreat — the secular clergy, as well as the members of religious families who, to Our pleasure, We have heard are to join in it. And We implore for them the motherly regard of the Most Holy Virgin and the aid of all

the Saints and elect who have besought and obtained by means
of the Spiritual Exercises a most intimate knowledge of Our
Lord, a most ardent love for Him, and a most unflagging
perfection in walking in His steps. We delegate you expressly
to impart Our Apostolic Benediction, the pledge of Our
paternal affection, to all who promote and take part in the
Week."

The significance of these papal documents issued at a critical
moment during the controversy on prayer can readily be ap-
prehended. They were not the first expressions of the great
Pontiff's high regard for the Exercises during his pontificate.
In July, 1922, acting on the petition of 672 bishops of both
rites throughout the Catholic world, Pius issued the Apostolic
Constitution, *Summorum Pontificum,* declaring and enacting
St. Ignatius to be the Patron Saint of retreats and retreat
houses everywhere. This enactment could have been made by
means of a simple decree of the Congregation of Rites or by
an Apostolic Brief. The Holy Father chose to give the document more importance by making it an Apostolic Constitution
to be promulgated like a Papal Bull. In it he alludes to the
high esteem in which the Ignatian method of prayer has been
held for three centuries by men distinguished for their dis-
ciplined and holy lives. Four saints are cited by name: St.
Francis de Sales, who prepared himself for the episcopacy
and planned his life by a study of the Exercises; St. Charles
Borromeo, who drew from them inspiration for a saintly career
and spread their use among clergy and laity; St. Teresa, "that
teacher of the highest contemplation"; and her spiritual son,
the Franciscan St. Leonard of Port Maurice, who affirmed
that he followed the method of St. Ignatius in gaining souls
to God. The Holy Father ends by saying that the Exercises
contain the solution of the problems peculiar to our times and
that it is his dearest wish to see the Exercises in use among
clergy, laity, and religious congregations, but especially among
the working classes.

In December of the same year, 1922, Pius sent an Apostolic Letter, *Meditantibus Nobis,* to the General of the Society on the occasion of the tercentenary of the canonization of St. Ignatius and St. Francis Xavier, in which he reiterates his commendation of the Exercises. In the course of it he says that other exercises of this kind are not to be lightly esteemed but those of St. Ignatius have enjoyed the special approbation of the Holy See because they are so wisely graduated, all the parts so closely knit, that they produce radical transformation in the soul and make it docile to authority: they offer a better hope, tested by long experience, of resulting in solid and lasting good.

CHAPTER II

THE NOVICE

IN THIS chapter I shall reproduce excerpts from the diary of a young Jesuit of modern date. He did not belong to the same Province of the Society as the one I am in. His papers came to me through a member of his family who has given me permission to publish extracts from them. Their only interest lies in the intimate glimpses of what is going on in the mind of the average Jesuit during the years of his formation. They are fairly representative of the little private business seriously conducted by every aspirant to worthy membership in the Society of Jesus. So much fantastic nonsense about the training and formation of the Jesuit has been obligingly fed to a public, avid for mystery and the sensational, by writers who do not mind what they say, that the view of a living specimen may be more enlightening than the popular museum specimens supplied by ill-instructed historians.

The first entry, dated a few months after entrance into the novitiate, runs: "I have tried to begin the new year well by faithfully keeping the rules of silence, modesty, etc. I have begun the habit of speaking Latin during free time; my perseverance and indifference to criticism will be put to the test in continuing the practice; but I hope to be able to continue, *Deo assistente*. I consider the cultivation of exterior and interior coolness in trying circumstances of special importance. That and a habit of politeness will be particularly noticed by me in the pages of this diary which I hope St. Ignatius will make a means of my becoming a better son of his."

Most of the entries that follow, covering with brief lapses a period of some years, are a chronicle of successes and failures, generally failures, in overcoming defects of character as they are brought out by the close contacts of a common life in a religious community.

"In after-dinner recreation I was heavy, probably on account of dinner. I was not so polite as I might have been, leaning my head on the table and speaking sententiously."

"I was the principal in the *exercitium modestiae* this evening." This is an exercise in which the master of novices, sitting at a table with the victim kneeling on the floor in front of him, asks the encircling novices what faults they noted in their fellow novice. "I received five admonitions: (1) Dragging feet in ascetery (the common room). (2) Tactus (touching others unnecessarily). (3) Speaking to members of other divisions. (4) Obstinacy in holding my own opinions. (5) Impatience. I must endeavor to pay special attention to these points."

"I did one mean thing on the walk today. I let another see that he was not welcome in the group in which I was. I will never do that again."

The midday dinner was probably a pleasant item in the order of the day; but apparently it made things harder afterwards. Again we find it blamed:

"I must have eaten too much dinner, for I was a little snappish in after-dinner recreation."

But later on a success is recorded, but minimized:

"I was comparatively affable and polite in recreation; but this was perhaps owing to my feelings which were just naturally good today. I had nothing to overcome. The true virtue of charity is exercised in overcoming ourselves in the practice of it."

Another triumph is recorded, but after supper:

"In after-supper recreation I managed to desist from self-defense against adverse criticism. I was about to object several times, but I am glad I did not."

"Today I had a long conference with the novice master. He said my resolutions to mind my own business and see less going on around me were a useful means of overcoming rash judgments and defects against charity. He said no one is more pernicious to the Society than the man who is not humble. I should do my best on all occasions but must afterwards refer everything to God. I should lead a supernatural life, all my motives and aims being founded on God and heaven. When my superiors, no matter who, ask me to do something, they may or may not have a good reason for it. But God has a good reason for it; and it may fall out that His reason may be different from the superior's. It is the safest course to obey promptly and without words. I have made good resolutions; now I hope they stick."

The diarist all through the year and succeeding years keeps recurring to the great need of charity and patience. He has a hard time of it. After noting some failure remorsefully he often ends with a prayer to the Sacred Heart or to our Lady: "To preserve a Jesuit's dignity, to treat others like brothers and gentlemen, to maintain interior peace, O Mother, give me patience, charity and self-denial."

"In my monthly conference I told the novice master I had great difficulty in practising common charity. He quietly told me how necessary it was; how in the colleges we would meet all sorts of characters, and how, if we found ourselves unable to get along with them and lose sight of ourselves for the sake of others, what trouble and discontent awaited us, not to speak of the small influence we would be able to wield in the interests of Christ and the Society. He said this briefly, simply, and every word carried conviction.

"I told him I could not help feeling a little deceitful when I concealed my real feelings and accommodated myself to the feelings and ideas of another at the sacrifice of private convictions. The holy man here made a distinction which struck me forcibly; which I never remember to have come across. Although, he said, in repressing and concealing our feelings, we show outwardly a calmness or pleasure which actually does not exist inside, and thus lay ourselves open apparently to the accusation of deceit or want of candor, such is not really the case. And he went on to explain. For instance, someone injures me: forthwith there arises a feeling of resentment and anger. At this point two spirits are contending for mastery in me: the spirit of evil and the spirit of good. One urges surrender to anger; the other counsels charity, imitation of Christ by conquering my anger and aversion and returning good for evil. One is my lower self; the other is my higher self. Why must it be deceit and want of candor to show my higher self? For a follower of Christ, if there is any deceit, it is in showing our lower self, hiding and denying the higher and truer self which it is our duty to cultivate and turn to the world at large.

"Then he said that we should lose sight of ourselves and our own interests and pleasure in striving to make others happy. The other novices have left home and loving families, and they expect to be recompensed in some degree by their brothers in Christ. They have their defects. Who has not? And why shouldn't they, coming directly from the world."

"I wish I could cultivate thoughtful habits. There is nothing so sure to make me uneasy, restless, discontented and shallow as this overflow of disjointed, aimless and wandering fancies. My mind chases every hare that starts up. 'Quanto aliquis magis sibi unitus et interius simplificatus est, tanto plura et altiora sine labore intelligit quia desuper lumen intelligentiae accipit.'"

"Here is a thought from Father Lallemant: Never let yourself entirely out. Always keep a surplus of self behind. At all times and in all moods retain a reserve force of self. Don't flow out like water. Don't be afraid of creating a false impression. If excess is in question, let it be on the side of silence.

"I made my manifestation today to Reverend Father Provincial. He was kind and gentle, and was a great help. With nations, he said, the general course of their history runs through the following succession: Peace, Prosperity, Pride, War, Humiliation. He said the same was true of individuals who followed the impulse of their emotions. When everything was going along to their satisfaction, they were not only happy but overbearing. But it took only a word or a look to raze their structure of contentment, and then they found themselves at odds with everybody and did foolish things and lost all peace of soul and became desolate and bitter. He advised me, when I felt that way, to speak familiarly to God somewhat as follows: O Lord, You see what a weak, foolish fellow I am. I need all the help You can give me, and I need it most when I forget You and think I can go along on my own resources. It is easy to go along without You when things run smoothly; and it is also easy to go along with You then; but going along with You when everything is fine does not mean much unless I forget myself. And that is precisely what I don't do. If I went along with You in the right way when everything was bright, I would not feel so forsaken and discouraged when everything became dark. You are with me in darkness as well as in brightness. Only I can show more trust in You, and more love, by refusing to be downcast and baffled and defeated, by beginning over again, more distrustful of self and more trustful of You. Father Provincial's example of familiar prayer was most inspiring, and I am going to practice it more."

Before taking his vows at the expiration of the two years of noviceship, the novice has a final conference with the novice master:

"We discussed several points. (1) Anxiety about the future, at being left to one's self for spiritual direction. I told him that he had called me so seldom for conferences that I thought his plan was to leave everyone to the promptings of the Holy Spirit. I said I had misgivings on this score as I frequently forgot myself and stood in need of constant reminders. The

N.M. acknowledged that he left everyone to himself as much as possible, that it was dangerous to interfere. He told me there was no need of fretting. The Society always provided ample means of sanctification for its members. The voice of the Holy Spirit will always make itself heard. The danger lies not in missing it, nor in failing to hear it distinctly, but in deliberately closing one's ears to it when it speaks loudly and distinctly. God is merciful. He deals out reminders abundantly, in sickness or disappointments or failures, etc. (2) Preoccupation with studies and a growing carelessness about spiritual things. I told him how weak and ephemeral my resolutions were. He urged me to practise having a pure intention in my work. He approved my idea of a diary. No matter how many times I broke the resolutions written down in my diary, it would work out all right in the end. I would have gained something even after a long record of failures, and in years to come the sad account would help me to be humble. (3) The possibility of leaving the Society. I told him the talk among the novices — how many Jesuits left after having taken their vows. This he denied. He said comparatively few left. A man, he said, is seldom dismissed from the Society, unless he is incorrigible. Two Jesuits might have the same faults in species and number and one might leave the Society on account of them. This need not be a cause for worry to the one who remained faithful; for the sole reason that he was docile and strove against his faults. (4) The difficulty of being open and frank with superiors. I told him I should probably be tongue-tied with my superiors. I was naturally secretive and reticent with persons I didn't know well. He said he understood and I need not force frankness. Silence and reticence became evil only when the man made up his mind to conceal his thoughts. As long as we are willing to tell everything but are really withheld by natural disposition, no danger can be reasonably anticipated. Finally I asked what special fault I ought in his estimation to guard against in the future. He bent his head and contracted his eyebrows in his thoughtful way, and after a few moments said as to faults he could not say very well, but he could give me some advice which would be valuable to me if I tried to follow it. He said I would be naturally inclined to misconstrue the words and action of others. Sometimes I might be right; but whether right or wrong, he said, always seem to forget the matter entirely and act afterwards as if nothing had happened to disturb me. In our interpretation of what others say and do, we are generally wide of the mark. Very often things were never intended in the light in which we saw them. At all times it would be the safe course, as it was the only right course, never to notice injuries real or imaginary. He said I would have frequent opportunities of following this advice."

"Today the novice master gave us a last talk before the taking of our vows. He said the day on which we said our First Mass, if it so pleased God, would be a happy day; but tomorrow laid claim to greater importance. He exhorted us in simple words to aim always at perfection. He said we would fall again and again, we would grow tepid and careless, but it should be our unwavering principle not to give way to discouragement and to rise again and try again. He said he hoped to hear of us as great Jesuits, or at least he hoped others would hear of us as such since he himself would in all probability be dead and gone."

In making these selections, more or less at random, it has been my purpose to give some idea of what occupies the novice's mind during his two years of probation. He is busy noting and correcting his defects, especially those which interfere with the harmonious conduct of community life; he is engaged in the difficult task of readjusting his outlook and way of living to supernatural principles; he is learning the necessity of habits of prayer in the acquirement and permanent possession of the supernatural point of view; he is absorbing from the rules, and Jesuit history and biography, and the traditions of the Province, whatever information he can get about the spirit of the Society; he is, in a word, learning the meaning of perfection according to Jesuit ideals, and ways of practicing it with the helps that the Society affords.

The diary, as I said, continues beyond the novitiate for some ten years. These were years busy with studies and teaching in the schools of the Society and with less leisure for self-study. But it is noteworthy that the entries continue to be of the same general color as in the noviceship, less concerned with external activities than with the progress of the spirit and the troublesome imperfections of a difficult nature. I do not think it is unusual for a Jesuit thus to keep a watchful eye on himself no matter how busy or conspicuous he may be in public employments. The Jesuit of Protestant and anticlerical tradition is a sinister devil engaged for some inconceivable reason in devious treasons against Church or State. He is undoubtedly much less interesting in his actual role of a poor sinner trying to save his soul in dangerous currents and haply reaching out a hand now and then to some struggling soul near by. It is, I suppose, hopeless to expect a secular literature to grasp the supernatural aims and machinery of any Religious Order, and specifically of the Jesuits. This is most regrettable. For, paradoxically, the less supernatural a Jesuit is made to appear, the more inhuman he will seem. And great literature ought to be able to make even a Jesuit human and intelligible.

CHAPTER 12

PIERRE BOUSCAREN

IN CHOOSING an instance of how the spirit of the Society manifests itself in the concrete, I suppose the best way would be to look among the canonized saints of the Society. It was the spirit of the Society that helped to make them saints; and they exemplify that spirit most triumphantly. This manner of selection, however, might not satisfy everybody. After all, comparatively few Jesuits have been canonized. How about the thousands that have not been canonized? It might be urged that the Saints have been the exception, whereas they ought to be the rule if the Society's spirit is operative in producing an exalted type of sanctity.

This objection has a certain measure of validity. But much of its force is lost when we stop to consider the nature of sanctity in its heroic degree and the conditions favorable to its official recognition by the authorities of the Church. The Society has to do the best it can with the material that comes to it. Not all that material is heroic stuff. While the mold to which it is subjected may be, and is, heroic enough, the human material is not always ready to receive the complete impression. It must be sufficiently ductile to receive some impression: otherwise it is rejected. In the difficult and supernatural art of holiness, aspiration is, in our fallen state, far more common than realization. At the same time, high aspiration is not without excellence in a world of low aims.

It is more than a matter of mere conjecture that in the long history of the Church innumerable saints of heroic stature have slipped away without having attracted attention outside their immediate circle. Sanctity is a secret process. How am I to know a man is a saint of canonizable dimensions? I may live with him for years. I may admire his scrupulous fidelity to every least obligation, his amiable manners, his hard work, his zeal and prudence, his love of prayer and retirement, his indifference to hardship, his patience in suffering. We are all convinced that his interior life must be that of a great saint, to be so fruitful of visible perfection. But he may be an old man now. All or most of his contemporaries are dead — those who were his confessors and spiritual guides and those who were his superiors, all those, in a word, who, when he comes to die, could testify to his virtue. He will leave no spiritual diary, nor will there survive any correspondence with intimate details of his soul. After he has gone, everyone will say, "A saint has gone out from among us." And that will be the end of it.

Divine Providence certainly has everything to do with the selection of saints for canonization. But to human eyes the official recognition of heroic sanctity seems to depend upon the conjuncture of what might be called happy accidents. It may be surmised that God thus arranges circumstances to bring out some new facet of His beauty and goodness for public veneration.

I need not say that I have nothing to do with the canonization of saints. Pierre Bouscaren, whom I select to exemplify the spirit of the Society, may or may not be submitted to the processes which determine a subject's fitness for the honors of the altar. My choice falls on him for the very reason that he has not been declared a saint, and may never be.

He was born in Cincinnati in 1889, two days before the new year, in a family that was prominent in the civic and social life of the city. His education was received at home and at St. Xavier's, the Jesuit school in his native city, which he attended for eight years. His school fellows described him as lively, alert, with ideas of his own, with no shy diffidence and with a singular indifference to the impression he might be making on others. He was a good student and came to know French as perfectly as his own tongue. During what would have been his last college year, he toured the old world in the company of his sister and aunt, visited the Pyramids, rowed on the Jordan, climbed to the top of Milan Cathedral and the ruins of the Villa Hadriana — like Watterton, the naturalist, he was not quite happy unless he found some place to climb. One hopes he did not drag his sister and his aunt along. In the brief sketch of his life which Father Garraghan prefixed to the small volume of diary notes and letters, published in 1935,* the following extract from young Pierre's unpublished travel journal (in three volumes) will give a notion of the sprightly character of the youth: "There were wood benches instead of chairs, and a delicious dog passes several times under our table, rubbing our legs to remind us that we were in a genuine trattoria; for no trattoria is complete, no trattoria has the proper Walter Scott air, unless it has a dog at table."

On his return from abroad, Pierre entered the Jesuit novitiate at Florissant, August 14, 1908. He was a stout lad of over six feet; but in his second year of novitiate he had hemorrhages of the lungs, and from that time till his death, nearly twenty years later, he was physically a broken man. He was not, however, the sort of man whom bad health and imminent death could browbeat. He yielded to none of the depressive forebodings of ill health. When good days came, he worked and prayed and practised austerities; and when the bad days came he took them in his stride and waited cheerfully for them to issue either way, in a return to activity or in final rest. Sick or well, he was the most buoyant of men. He followed with more than ordinary success the regular courses of classics, philosophy and theology, most of the time on a sickbed, and after his tertianship was appointed professor of philosophy in the Jesuit house of studies in St. Louis. Besides teaching philos-

---

* Bruce, Milwaukee.

ophy, he was the spiritual director of the young Jesuits, gave the regular community instructions, acted as chaplain to the Little Sisters of the Poor, and preached retreats to religious communities, one of them being a retreat of thirty days. The ailment that had been dogging him for nearly twenty years had its way at last. On Christmas day, 1927, St. Louis lay under a pall of smoke and fog painful to respiratory organs. Father Bouscaren was prostrated, but only physically. To a visitor in his sickroom who spoke a word of sympathy for his suffering, he said, "This is the happiest Christmas I have ever spent. Somehow or other I never felt closer to our Lord than I feel today." In the course of the day the doctor advised that he be removed to the clearer air of the country, and he was taken to Florissant. In his comatose condition, courtesy prompted the few words he spoke. They were words of thanks to those who were assisting him. He died early that evening.

To the world at large and to his brethren, Father Pierre was a big man of expansive manners and exuberant energy. His associates knew his large stature was not a sign of robust health: they often saw him suffering and brought low by his chronic disease. But they never detected the usual betrayals of the semi-invalid, impatience, querulousness, cowardice in meeting the demands of life, pettishness, gloomy moods, and the eager quest for refuge in small comforts. Father Bouscaren seemed to welcome his distressing periods of inaction; and, when he was on his feet again, he increased rather than diminished his activity. His zeal for God's work was obvious to all: he never tried to disguise or conceal it. With great keenness of intellect and the most exalted spiritual ideals, he was forbearing and gentle and unassuming. Everyone could infer from the daily aspect of his perfect manner — his joyful observance of every little requirement of the religious life, his almost hilarious cheerfulness, his infectious enthusiasm for holy causes, and his unselfish and untiring devotion to them — anyone could infer that behind it all there must be an interior spiritual life of an extraordinary kind. His confessor and his superiors knew it. For the rest of us, it remained a matter of vague certainty until some extracts from his spiritual journal and several of his letters were published eight years after his death.

I shall select a few of the more significant passages from the published material.

Tuesday, August 31, 1909. During his novitiate. "How good God is to me. I must serve Him with all my strength. I must do my level best to be a saint. Anything that I do tends to my sanctification. I must call to mind before each act: 'This is to help to my sanctification.' In this spirit must I rise promptly, dress quickly, use my time well before meditation, make my meditation with all the earnestness of my soul, hear Mass devoutly and with confidence, i.e., expecting from it that Christ will help me to my sanctification no matter what aridity I feel; receive Communion with the same confidence and ardent desire for perfection; wait at table, take meals, do my work, make spiritual reading, go through class, take recreation, use free time, trying to do each thing perfectly."

All the entries are notes jotted down after his morning meditation to remind him of the resolutions made in it. They nearly all revolve around his general purpose of making himself a saint. In one entry he has a list of his defects, as they were pointed out by his fellow novices in the *exercitium modestiae*. Contrary to the common notion of Jesuit ways, there was nothing secret or underhand about it. "I answer litanies too fast. When I wait on others at table, I do so with too much show of eagerness; I reach too far at table for dishes. I ask unnecessary and vague questions in class, and seem at times to impolitely dispute correctness of what teacher has said; appear absentminded during recreation, wait to laugh at jokes; hold head on one side and stretch neck; start too suddenly at sound of bell; inconvenience others by my elbows. Father Rector tells me I must have more discretion, tells me to rejoice at chance to

practice the 11th rule of Summary." As Father Hornsby, who
edits the journal, observes in a footnote, "It will be noticed
that there is no mention made of any serious fault, such as
violations of charity, want of promptness, and the like."

"Day of My Vows. Thursday, September 8, 1910. (Pierre
had been prevented by illness from taking his vows on
August 15, and needed to be supported in the chapel while
taking them. He makes no mention of his condition.) God
almighty, everlasting made me and gave me all I have. How
just is it that I should give it all back to Him, give Him myself and my all. I belong to Him hereafter. I'll take no delight
in anything of the earth, in comforts, pleasures, praises. My
greatest delight will be to suffer the contrary of these, that I
may be better assured that I am with my Lord. 'If anyone
will come after me,' etc."

In the first year of his studies, he made a resolution, which
he renewed annually, to observe the rules as if, like Blessed
Claude de la Colombiére, he had taken a vow never to violate
the least of them. "December 12, 1912. . . . Every time a harsh
thought, implying a harsh judgment of one of my dear
brothers, comes to my unworthy little mind, I will raise my
heart to my Master and say, 'Lord, be Thou praised in all
Thy servants: help my brother, and give me grace to see my
own many faults, and not to see the little faults of Thy friends
with whom Thou dost allow me to live, and who so charitably
bear with me.' . . . I will avoid loud talking and the delivering
of quasi-dissertations. I will avoid gestures that attract attention. As to contention, if I find myself engaged in it, I will
uncompromisingly catch the first possibility to drop it, by
ceding the point, or in some other way.

"Palm Sunday, March 16, 1913. . . . During the novena in
honor of St. Francis Xavier, I asked him to obtain purity for
me, and in fact I have felt fewer temptations against this virtue
since then, but I have felt wretched temptations to vanity and
contempt of my brethren, and I have been distracted by idle

thoughts when I wished to be recollected. That's what I have of my own. My heart is filled with miserable beasts of this kind, which show their heads sometimes, to let me see how detestable I am. It's my cross to see my bad inclinations, to be humbled by their consideration, and to be obliged always to combat them. My dear Lord will never leave me without some cross or humiliation. When He frees me from one of my passions, He will permit me to discover some other, until He gives me the grace to be entirely humble of heart, and gives me great suffering of body and soul to bear for Him.

"Saturday, May 19, 1913. . . . My Lord still tells me that I am not sufficiently united with Him. . . . I am too dissipated in recreation; I do not lower and despise myself enough. . . . I must be too serious, too recollected to permit myself to get angry in recreation. . . . I should not be so fond of laughing and joking, of speaking of things which are not directly concerned with the knowledge, love, and service of God. I may speak of indifferent things, of sciences, studies, etc., if it's inevitable or necessary; but that must always be with less enjoyment and pleasure than when I speak of the things of God; and whatever be the subject of my conversation, I must always remain united with God and often raise my heart to Him. I must not, moreover, permit so much liberty to my eyes as before. There are a thousand things that I have no need to see. A look that may be of some little use, by letting me know something of little importance, costs me much more than it profits me, by depriving me of union with God.

"Sunday, June 8, 1913. I asked my Spiritual Father if it would be well for me to prostrate myself on the floor to adore God, and to kiss the feet of our Lord and the Blessed Virgin, to kiss the floor during my prayer. He said: 'No,' my devotion ought not to be mixed with affections of the flesh; there is danger in that. Well, then, my dear Saviour forbids me what I thought a holy sweetness. May His will be done. 'Only Thy love and Thy grace.'

"September 20, 1913. . . . I want to be a saint."

"March 28, 1914. Friday evening I had a good conference with Father Hagemann. I told him that I had ideas perhaps a little too fixed on the uselessness of keeping up with what is going on in the world; that I did not find it necessary to keep up by reading such periodicals as *America* and the *Scientific American;* that I had no time to do so; that, even if I had the time and could not employ it better, I was afraid that those things would impede my recollection; that I would prefer to go to the colleges to teach, without information on the topics of the day than go without being a good religious, without having the spirit and habit of recollection, without having learned to think, without being so well founded in the sciences which it is my duty to study now, without having the spirit of prayer, union with God, piety, mortification, and work. That information, I said, I can pick up in a short while at any time and without much trouble; but the solid virtues, solid sciences I cannot acquire but with long time and at the expense of constant efforts. The Father said that I was entirely right. 'I was afraid, Father,' I said, 'that there was danger of becoming too much of a hermit.' 'There is no danger,' he answered, 'of becoming too good a religious.'

"April, 1914. . . . Let my Lord do with me what He will. Let Him give me a crown of thorns to wear if He wishes. I have frequently offered Him all my body and soul, all my members, all my organs. To show me that He accepted it all, He has deigned to come down and take one of my lungs. . . . In giving back my health, He asks me not to die, but that which is much harder — to live for Him. . . . My time, all my faculties, every effort in studies and other work and in my spiritual life — all belongs to Him. Let Him make me feel inspiration and enthusiasm if He will. But I can get along without them if He wishes me to do so. One thing only, I desire; that is to love Him always more and more, and to serve Him always better and better."

These are brave words; but they were not idle words, the expression of an imaginary heroism unrelated to realities. In July of this year, Pierre had severe hemorrhages. He was thought to be dying and received Extreme Unction. For the two following years he was an invalid, confined to a bed most of the time, with much suffering to undergo and unable to continue his studies. But his spiritual journal was kept up, and we learn from it that, far from finding his sickness an excuse for relaxation, he made it serve spiritual ends and found it most precious in bringing him closer to our Lord. The following entry was made while he was a patient at Mount St. Rose, a tuberculosis sanatorium in St. Louis:

"Monday, August 24, 1914. . . . Now He has put me among His suffering brothers. How it tears one's heart to hear the groaning and moaning and coughing at night. Here are men who suffer more than I, and they are the little children of our Lord, poor, weak children, while I am the brave knight who has given himself to His service. Why does He not take all this suffering from His little children to give it to me who should bear it? May He do His will, and may He give me grace always to do my duty loyally, generously, and with the greatest love."

"Wednesday, July 4, 1917. Our Lord has not yet given our dear country a saint among its children. If He wishes to give one, whoever is chosen must cooperate. I will not leave the cooperation to others."

The reader will note the date of this entry: Independence Day, with its noisy celebration of fireworks and patriotic speeches. I venture to say that few lovers of their country expressed their love in the manner of Pierre.

Throughout the journal, Pierre often refers to his sins and imperfections in a way that might be misleading to a reader not familiar with the language of holiness. The next entry from which I quote may be enlightening.

"Thursday, April 4, 1918. Today I have made a little retreat of one day, speaking as little as possible, and giving all my time to prayer. . . . Our Lord goes up the mountain; those who wish follow Him. They are not obliged to follow Him up there, for He is ready to preach to those also who are in the plain. . . . He called me to the mountain, or rather He permitted me to see and go up. He encouraged me to be bold in my ambition, and now, after ten years, I can say that He has not disappointed me. I have desired religious perfection, fidelity to duty, the cross. . . . He has given me His grace. I have been faithful to Him in spite of my imperfections: I do not think that I have ever offended Him mortally. I have done my duty; I have been obedient; for eight years I have borne the cross of sickness, which seemed so heavy in the beginning. This cross and all sufferings have become sweet to me. My vocation, my vows, and everything connected with the perfection of a Jesuit, is sweeter to me now than ever, even if the custom of years renders this sweetness a little less sensible. Truly, my Saviour has quite justified my daring. . . . He encourages me to be still more daring in the future, more daring and more generous."

For some years Pierre had made sacramental confession a daily practice. Just before his ordination, he asked and obtained from his spiritual adviser permission to go to confession twice a day. Those who lived with him thought it was because he expected a sudden death. His journal gives another explanation.

"December, 1918. . . . It would give me the grace of the sacrament twice as often, and would be a powerful aid to attain that absolute purity of conscience which I wish to have as a priest. This is a little unusual, it is true, but it is in keeping with the recommendation made to priests in their rules to go to confession oftener than once a week; no one need know what I am doing except my confessor. Finally, I don't feel the least danger of falling into scruples in the matter; my confessions have never been an occasion of scruples for me; on the contrary, they have been a sensible source of strength and encouragement. In asking of our Lord pardon of my sins in the sacrament each time I examine my conscience, I shall be better protesting to Him that I am entirely resolved to serve Him perfectly, and I shall keep this determination more lively in my mind."

In his annual retreat of 1920, he notes, "During the second week I felt the sweetest tenderness of love for my Master and Lord Jesus Christ, tenderness the like of which I have not felt for a long time except for a brief space. I received it with all the force of my will, and I profited by it to make the intensest and strongest possible acts of love for my Saviour. I thought that thus I might make reparation for the indeliberate sins of the flesh which I have no doubt committed."

The pages of his spiritual notes are filled with his love of suffering and voluntary penances. "Thursday, August 11, 1921. I have begun the practice of making vows, binding under pain of mortal sin, to do penances, and I believe that this is pleasing to our Lord, as it increases the merit of the penances. My Spiritual Father approves, provided I do not make such vows too often. I also ask my confessor from time to time to give me a particular penance, such as to take the discipline or wear the chain, or to say the penitential psalms on my knees. He approves of the practice. I follow it because works done as a sacramental penance are more meritorious than those done without obligation. I shall never be able to suffer enough or do enough for my Saviour. Oh, if He would grant me to be roasted alive for Him as St. Lawrence."

About a year later: "I feel a very passionate love for the most sacred Humanity of our Lord Jesus Christ. I ask Him to make me entirely His and inflict upon me the severest suffering, to purify and sanctify my love for Him and so increase it without end. I like to inflict pain on myself."

Father Bouscaren's Provincial must have adverted dubiously to this liking of self-inflicted pain, for we find him writing to the Provincial in July, 1923, in explanation. "As to my attraction to severity, I fear certain expressions of my last letter may have conveyed a wrong impression. The desire for penance and severity does not dominate my spiritual life. It is love for our Lord and the desire to testify my love and to glorify Him that dominates me. I am impelled to do this in the enduring of physical pain, of fatigue, of disappointments, of interior and exterior humiliations, and of reprehensions, and in forcing myself to the carrying out of duties that are against my taste. I find nothing so efficacious to excite my love, to humiliate me, and to drive me to the performance of repugnant duty, as the taking of the discipline. Other external penances appeal to me for the same reasons, and so the desire of corporal and spiritual pain is continually before me; but I always make it a point of conscience to have a constant regard for prudence, and I often make my offering to our Lord consist in foregoing the penance I desire to do. I have asked advice in the matter, both from the doctor and from the Spiritual Father, and I sincerely believe I have been quite sufficiently prudent. Whatever I do in this line is done in the spirit of the greatest joy and the most complete liberty of conscience. . . . My sense of sinfulness is considerable, but has no suggestion of morbidity . . . it is only an aspect of my love for Christ, and is not nearly so strong as it might well be: I hope it will become stronger when the Spirit of God moves me in that direction. At present His impulse seems to be rather to His love in its other aspects.

"I know that the free expression of such sentiments is liable to abuse, and that when encouraged it may well become miasmic. I will try to observe propriety, and I believe you will show me the paternal kindness of repression when you judge repression opportune."

During the last years, Father Bouscaren, while teaching philosophy to the young Jesuits, was also their Spiritual Father. In May of the year in which he died, he wrote, "May we all contribute to the full extent of our power, to the sanctification of the whole Society. The more intimately I come to know the souls and hearts of our younger brethren, the more I admire the rich potentialities for sanctity which our Lord has prepared and given the Society." His first year as a teacher of philosophy was not so successful as it was to be in the following years. This accomplished man — the spiritual notes from which we have been quoting were written, as inclination moved, in lucid English, French, and Latin — did not hesitate to ask the young men in his class to point out his defects as a teacher. Father Hornsby gives us an amusing excerpt from one of the criticisms, covering two pages, which was preserved among Father Bouscaren's notes. It ends with this word of encouragement: "You can be a first-class teacher if you do as I have directed. Everyone says that you 'could' be, but that you aren't now, simply because of faults that are correctible." Another sentence places the young mentor in a better light: "One thing you do, Father, makes you a success anyway; that is, you make us all love God more. Let that console you for the past."

An incident like this would indicate that Father Bouscaren's intensely spiritual life had not made him aloof and unapproachable. His journal, letters, and notes show his efforts to cultivate a congenial manner. "The mildness and imperturbably benevolent attitude of our Tertian Master has made me ashamed of my rigor and austerity. I am trying to carry out the program to make my sanctity attractive, and to make it the inspiration to myself of suffering in the active life, and I think I am finding my way to this." In one of the entries in 1923, he writes: "I have been thinking a great deal for the past month of the excellence we should aim at — in spirituality, in the acquisition of learning and erudition, and in good manners, and I have felt no little indignation against those who seem to neglect this threefold excellence."

In view of his infirm health, it is rather incongruous to find him writing to his Provincial and begging to be sent to the foreign missions or assigned to work among the colored people. But I shall return to this latter in another chapter.

CHAPTER 13

THE JESUIT LAY BROTHER

JESUIT lay brothers are not mere Jesuit auxiliaries: they are Jesuits in every sense of the word. They take vows and share in all the spiritual life and spiritual privileges of the society. They enter the Society to be lay brothers and to serve in the lower branches of the religious establishment, attending to its material needs and helping to create those domestic conditions which are favorable to study, prayer, and the free exercise of the Society's ministry in all its various forms. They have no part in the government of the Society and are comparatively seldom called upon to assume secretarial and similar duties or to use a special talent unless it is of practical utility. It is evident that the Jesuit lay brother's lot is from a worldly point of view a humble lot.

But it would be a grave error, however, to conclude that his lot is insignificant as well as humble. We must not forget that in the Society spiritual values have the first place. The first question in the Society is, Is he a spiritual man? Not, Is he a learned man? or a competent man? or a brilliant man? Those questions may be asked; but they are not the first to be asked. And a lay brother can become a very spiritual man indeed. There are four lay brothers among the twenty-three canonized saints of the Society; and, among the 126 Jesuits who have been beatified, twenty-two are lay brothers. In evaluating these statistics it is to be remembered that the number of lay brothers in the Society at any time is far fewer than that of priests and scholastics.

Alphonsus Rodriguez was canonized more than three hundred years after his death. He is the one confessor-saint among Jesuit lay brothers, that is, he was declared a saint by the Church simply because he lived the life of a Jesuit lay brother perfectly. Father Gerard Manley Hopkins wrote a sonnet on the occasion of the brother's canonization, in which he describes how the grace of God operates in the making of some of His saints. The poet usually "loaded his rifts with ore" to the confusion of the average reader of poetry. Although, in submitting the poem to Robert Bridges for criticism, he apologised with impatience for aiming to be intelligible, I shall take the liberty of giving the sequence of his thought before I quote him. I do not like to think of what he might have said if he knew someone was to aim to make it still more intelligible.

The sonnet begins by saying that honor, as commonly understood, is something arrived at by external acts. The visible scars of conquest blazon abroad the glory of the hero. It is thus with the wounds of Christ, as it is with those who openly and before the eyes of the world sacrificed their lives for Him by the sword of persecution. But, when the contest with the powers of darkness is waged in the secret recesses of the soul with unseen weapons and under cover of a drearily commonplace life, there is nothing to win attention and applause. God, however, works in manifold ways. Sometimes with bold strokes He hews out mountains and continents, stars and planets; sometimes He proceeds quietly and secretly in slow and minutely graduated steps as when He produces the delicately veined flowers of spring and the imperceptible growth of tall trees. In this silent way He worked His wonders in the soul of Alphonsus. During those forty years which the lay brother spent as porter at the door of the Jesuit college in Majorca, every day was lit with the splendor of hidden heroisms slowly fashioning the exquisite perfection of the Saint.

With this introduction, I give the poem:

"Honor is flashed off exploit, so we say;
  And those strokes once that gashed flesh or galled shield
  Should tongue that time now, trumpet now that field
  And, on the fighter, forge his glorious day.
  On Christ they do and on the martyr may;
  But be the war within, the brand we wield
  Unseen, the heroic breast not outward-steeled,
  Earth hears no hurtle then from fiercest fray.

"Yet God (that hews mountain and continent,
  Earth, all, out; who, with trickling increment,
  Veins violets and tall trees makes more and more)
  Could crowd career with conquest while there went
  Those years and years by of world without event
  That in Majorca Alfonso watched the door."

The will of our Creator is the most important thing in the world, and trying to learn it and do it is everybody's most peremptory business. Whether we do it in small things or big things is minor and irrelevant: it is probably harder to do it in the small things which familiar frequency has robbed of novelty and the excitement of summoning our resources for supreme effort. On the other hand it is easier to know God's will in the small things. God is closer to us when life is made up of simple elements. It is the "common people" that keep God in His world where it seems to be the ambition of uncommon people to cast Him out. Men who are caught up in the complex and swirling currents of affairs often have lucid moments when they dream of extricating themselves, when they feel that the world is too much with them and they yearn for a life reduced to its simplest denomination. There is not much room for nonsense, make-believe, and self-deception when the only problems we are called upon to solve are simple and elemental. This truth was not unknown to the old pagan philosophers.

In the light of this natural philosophy it is clear that the lay brother enjoys superior spiritual advantages. His employments are usually such as save him from the catastrophe of an idolatrous self-esteem. It is true, human nature can find outlets everywhere for its unruliness, and the porter at the door can stagger under the heavy burden of his own importance; but he does it in the face of great discouragements. When it comes to that supreme and essential rule of life laid down in the Ignatian meditation on the "Two Standards," that the true follower of Christ must court humility and obscurity above all things, the lay brother has everything in his favor. Those labors have the best chance of being carried on for the glory of God, in which there is little or no promise of glory for the laborer. A bright student, an eloquent preacher, an able executive, a distinguished educator or writer, is likely to be haunted by the uneasy doubt as to whether he is working for the glory of God or for his own glory. The more spiritual he is, the more he envies the lot of the lay brother.

In the patterning of one's life on that of Christ, it helps to have a clear and vivid picture of Him in our mind as we go through our daily occupations. Here the lay brother's advantage is obvious. The man who teaches analytic geometry to a reluctant class, or is giving a course in Elizabethan literature, or is maintaining discipline and struggling to preserve high standards in a large school, may sometimes have his doubts as to how Christ would do it. It is far easier to see Him helping Joseph in the carpenter's workshop and assisting His mother in the work of the house. The greater part of Christ's life was spent in these simple and homely employments.

A very fine Catholic poet in far-off New Zealand, Eileen Duggan, has put this thought into a beautiful poem on "Lay-Brothers."

"You are the hands of Christ, His calloused hands,
    Blistered and horny from the saw and plane.
    Before they, in their mercy, saved a pain,
    They pulled a heavy boat in on the sands.
    They were for use, His strong and able hands.

"You are the feet of Christ, His tired feet.
Let others show His mind — you have the best.
You go rough-shod like Him upon His quest.
He had to walk on foot through sun and sleet;
Save on Palm Sunday, He employed His feet.

"You are the mates of Christ, His dearest friends,
With whom He loves to sit and yarn awhile.
A working man is surest of His smile,
And He will say to you when living ends:
Come make yourselves at home My friends — My friends."

CHAPTER 14

EASTERN WINDOWS

I N HIS painstaking and spirited life of Father Eusebio Kino, S.J., entitled *The Rim of Christendom,* Professor Bolton quotes a characteristic passage from one of Father Kino's letters. Father Kino was a man of unusual talents. "He was," says Bolton, "great as a missionary, church-builder, explorer, ranchman, Indian diplomat, cartographer, and historian." As a young student in Europe, he showed great promise, and his superiors were reluctant to give him to the work in foreign missions for which he yearned. He wrote, at seven different times, long begging letters to the Father General, urging to be sent to China or any difficult mission field. "It was always a most agreeable pleasure to me," he wrote in later life to a friend, "to live in the rooms of our college where windows looked to the East, so that I might be comforted, at times oft-repeated during the day, by the mere sight of the East."

Father Kino's persistence finally won the day. He was sent however, not to China, but to Mexico. I think all readers of Professor Bolton's book will agree that China might have been the less arduous and dangerous of the two. Kino had his eyes upon the outposts as soon as he landed in Mexico; and then, not content with the outposts, he looked around for something harder and more perilous. He heard of California. The only California known at that time was Lower California, so poor in natural resourses that neither the Government in Spain nor its representatives in Mexico wanted anything to do with it. Its forsaken condition was the very reason Kino and his fellow missioner, Salvatierra, found most attractive. After years of effort the two missionaries succeeded in being charged by their superiors with the task of converting the natives of California. It had to be done without subsidies or aid from the Government.

"Thus," writes Hubert Howe Bancroft, the historian of the Southwest, and quoted by Bolton, "the boon, so long and patiently sought, was obtained — permission to enter, at their own risk and cost, a poor and unattractive country for the purpose of converting the heathen." And Bancroft goes on to make the following reflection: "It has been the fashion to see sinister and selfish designs in all Jesuit undertakings: but . . . no just person will suspect that the founders of California were actuated by any but the purest motives."

The young Jesuits of the new Society still gaze with longing eyes out of the eastern windows. I studied theology with a Spanish Jesuit who had been assigned to the Philippines about the time they were passing into the control of the United States. Those who are familiar with scholastic schools will know what a brilliant scholar he was when I tell them that he was chosen to make the Grand Act at the completion of his course. He was, moreover, a man of distinguished presence and affable manners. He thought I could help him in learning the English language and we were often together. His favorite topic was the missions. I pretended to throw cold water on his enthusiasm by assuring him that he would see very little of the rough and solitary life of mission work among savage people; that he would be a rector and superior all his life. He found that kind of talk most depressing. He told me what he wanted; the one thing he was praying for was to be sent to some remote and forlorn mission and to have sufficient physical strength to last on it ten years.

He went to the Philippines after his Grand Act, and, of course, became Rector of the college in Manila and Superior of the mission. Our feeble correspondence lapsed completely after a few years and I lost sight of him. About fifteen years later, while I was staying for a few days at Notre Dame University, I met one of the American missionary bishops returning from the Philippines. He was telling us of the hardships of the missions in the more remote parts of the Islands, and he singled out one especially for its remoteness from civilization and for the absence of everything that a civilized man comes to need. He spoke in awe and admiration of the missionary in charge of the station. It was my companion in theology. I heard afterwards that he was recalled to Spain; probably before the expiration of the ten years he had prayed for. If he were still in Spain, and living, I am sure, he was looking for a chance to add his name to the long roll of Jesuits who were in recent years the victims of anti-Christian persecution.

I am going to quote here from a long letter written by Father Pierre Bouscaren to his Provincial, in which he volunteers for the foreign missions. A short account of Father Bouscaren can be found in another chapter of this book. His letter will furnish unconsciously a ludicrous commentary on the "fashion of seeing sinister and selfish designs in all Jesuit undertakings."

Father Bouscaren begins his letter by acknowledging frankly his infirmities "of body and soul." In spite of these, he wishes to urge some strong reasons for believing that mission work is his divinely destined field. "First of all, I have always been attracted to the foreign missions, because of the hardships there are in them, because of the extreme need heathendom has, and because of our Lord's ever pressing appeal to teach all nations, to preach the Gospel to every creature, to save what is lost, and not to forsake the less favored sheep. Our Lord's pitiful call for helpers is always in the world and it seems to me that, if I want to answer it, He will give me the power somehow to do what I seek to do for Him.

"Then there is the desire for suffering with which He has inspired me. . . . Ever since my novitiate I have wanted to ask our Lord for the cross and for increase of suffering, but it was not until two years ago that I could get any spiritual director to approve of my making such a prayer. . . . During the past two

years I have asked for suffering outright, repeatedly, almost in-
cessantly, and with all the earnestness of my will; and I do not
think that our Lord, having given me the desire for so many
years, is going to deny me its fulfillment. . . . If I haven't the
physical strength or the other gifts to accomplish anything external on the missions, there is one thing that I can surely
accomplish with God's grace, namely, suffering — and there are
missions on which a healthy man can do no more than suffer and
perish. Xavier did not convert a single heathen by throwing
away his life at Sancian in a humanly hopeless undertaking;
but the moral and spiritual effects of his sacrifice have probably
been greater in the last four centuries than would have been
the fruit of twenty or thirty more years of even his prodigious
work. God seems to have chosen the suffering and disappointment and death of His servants as means for the accomplish-
ment of works which He does not will to accomplish by the
granting of immediate results. Is there no field in the world
where a few such deaths are needed now? And can I not die
as well with feeble health as with sound? . . . I have no
morbid desire to die. On the contrary, I feel a strong desire to
live as long as possible in order to do something for Christ in
action or in suffering or both; but I had rather live intensely for
six months than live a life of remiss devotedness for sixty
years. . . .

"I think my capability to bear physical fatigue is growing.
Until it becomes sufficient for the more arduous work, I might
devote myself to writing for the missions, and meantime pre-
pare myself by study. I already speak and write French, and
read Italian and Spanish with perfect fluency; and I am certain
that as soon as I take up consecutive reading in Portuguese —
which I intend to do very soon, in the letters of Francis Xavier
—I shall read it without difficulty. I expect to make a beginning with Polish next month, with a little help from Mr.
Zamiara, and when I have that it will probably be easy to
acquire Russian or other Slavic languages. . . . I do not want

to impede the action of Providence. If It wills to apply me to some other work than that of the missions, I will do with all devotedness whatever I am told, drawing inspiration from the thought that I am of one army with the men who hold parts of the field where there is daily challenge to heroism. I know that I shall be actually cooperating with them, since the whole Society is but one organism.

"Please excuse the length of this letter. I have presumed to write to you at such length because I wanted to open my heart to you as perfectly as possible. I have prayed particularly for light on this matter for about a month: I began writing the day before yesterday, the last day of the triduum; and I am ending on the feast of Blessed John Baptist Machado and Companions. I commend the matter to these martyrs, to Blessed Andrew Bobola, and to the Blessed Virgin. The intense desire and joy that I have felt in writing and meditating on this subject during the three days is likely enough, I think, to be some indication of Christ's choice. But I think no particular call is needed: the fact that I am of the Society is sufficient to warrant my volunteering." Father Bouscaren has a postscript at the end of the letter in which he says he kept it by him for five days before posting it, to make the matter "a subject for further meditation and prayer."

I am not concerned to prove that the missionary spirit among Jesuits is as active and heroic now as it ever was in the old Society. It is my opinion that it is. All I wish to show is that the Jesuit spirit, as manifested by eagerness to be sent to posts of danger and hardship on the missions, is still operating as of old. I have chosen my instances from those which lay, so to speak, at my own door. I could, if I wished, draw up a very impressive list of modern Jesuits whose hardihood in difficult mission fields imitates, if it does not rival, the heroism of their forefathers. But the only effect of such an enumeration might be to create the suspicion that these distinguished names are, after all, comparatively few and that they are very exceptional cases. By confining myself to my own immediate field of observation, which can be duplicated in every Province of the Society, I am more likely, I think, to succeed in conveying a truer impression.

In pursuing this plan, I shall here give a brief account of another missioner whom I knew. William Stanton entered the Society in 1887 from St. Louis where he had been educated at the Jesuit college. Following the regular course of a Jesuit scholastic at that time, he had five years of teaching, two of which were spent at the newly opened Jesuit college in Belize, British Honduras. This mission field had shortly before been assigned to the Missouri Province; it consisted of a number of stations in the interior among Maya Indians with headquarters in Belize. The prevalent languages were Spanish and Mayan although the colony belonged to England. During the school vacations Stanton made excursions to remote mission centers, most of them, on account of jungles and navigably uncertain rivers, difficult of access from Belize. He was a born explorer and naturalist, with an athletic turn, who took delight in the hazards and inconveniences of the wilderness. But, while he had a lively interest in fauna and flora and Mayan origins, what interested him most was the forsaken condition of the natives, their poverty and their need of religious instruction. When he returned to St. Louis to complete his studies, he had his mind made up to go back and try to do something for the Indians of British Honduras if he could get his superiors to agree.

At the end of his second year of theology, it looked as if his ambition was to be thwarted. The United States had taken over the Philippines from Spanish control. The famous observatory in Manila, in charge of Father Algue and his fellow Jesuits, was made a government institution, with the Jesuit director and his staff remaining at their posts. Application was made for an American Jesuit suitable for the work of the observatory who could act as interpreter and contact man with the American officials. Because of his knowledge of Spanish and his scientific attainments, Stanton was selected and sent to Manila. He had to get in somehow the year of theology still remaining before he could be ordained. This he succeeded in doing, besides performing brilliant work in the observatory and teaching English in the Ateneo, the old Jesuit college in Manila.

Father Stanton was the first American priest to be ordained in the Philippines. His activity after ordination grew incredibly. The cholera broke out among civilians and soldiers; the military chaplain died, the only other English-speaking priest in Manila. Father Stanton assumed his work among the soldiers and took charge of a parish church in the city. He ministered to the victims of the epidemic and rounded up the Catholic soldiers for confession and Sunday Mass. After the cholera had disappeared, he continued to look for every opportunity of exercising his priestly office. On the long inspection trips through the Islands, which his duties at the observatory required, he did whatever he could to supply the spiritual needs of the natives. Father William T. Kane, S.J., who wrote a most interesting life of Father Stanton, gives us some of the letters written at this time and goes on to say, "Yet one would scarcely gather from them how intensely active Stanton was at this time. With characteristic modesty he says nothing at all of his decidedly striking achievements in the field of science. It is almost incredible to find from the records of the Smithsonian Institution at Washington that, in the midst of a lot of other work, he discovered sixty-seven new varieties of hymenopterous insects, of which one genus and eight species have been named after him. . . . He wrote monographs on *Insects Affecting Crops in the Philippines,* in connection with his *Crop Service.* He made interesting and valuable researches in botany. With all this, and with a great deal of routine work in the observatory, he had a large task of smoothing, rather unofficially, the relations between the Government executives and the Fathers in charge of the Observatory. And he still found time for a multitudinous correspondence."

In 1904, after three years in Manila, Father Stanton was sent to Spain for his tertianship in Manresa, where St. Ignatius had written the "Spiritual Exercises." Here Father Stanton passed a fervent year. I shall not dwell upon it. All through this year he had been receiving letters from Father Algue and high American officials urging him to return as soon as possible to Manila. I have been told by Jesuits, who succeeded him there, that he was undoubtedly the most popular man in the Islands when he left them to go to Spain. And, for anyone who knew him, it is a report easy to believe. He had with a touch of courtliness a free and easy way of meeting everyone. His speech had something of the drawl we associate with the South, and this note was carried on in a certain indolence of manner. With his eyeglasses perched precariously on his nose, a slightly quizzical and humorous glint in his eyes, something of languor in his movement, he could have been the ornament of a select country club. Few could guess that he was a powerful swimmer, an indefatigable naturalist, an intrepid explorer, and a man burning with religious zeal. It is not surprising that those who had come to know him in Manila were eager to have him return.

But he never returned. He had not forgot the destitution of the Indians in British Honduras. At the end of his tertianship he wrote to his Provincial begging to be sent to them, saying "that our Lord, when on earth, had always had the keenest eye out for the chap who was in most need." And so it was decided that he was to found a new mission in the Cayo district of British Honduras among the abandoned tribes of Maya and Lacandon Indians. Thus Father Stanton voluntarily exchanged a mission field, where his talents and engaging manners could find great opportunity, for an obscure life of almost hopeless toil among a people less civilized than any to be found in the Philippines. The casual way in which he made his choice known to his Provincial was characteristic. The missionary spirit beneath was akin to that of Xavier and Jogues.

Father Stanton lasted just four years in the wilds of British Honduras. He had to be a strong man to last as long as that in the way he spent himself. At the time of his appointment he wrote: "What greater favor could the Lord bestow on me than to choose me for such apostolic work? And what greater joy for a son of Ignatius and a brother of Francis Xavier and Peter Claver and a thousand other missionaries of the Society, than to be allowed to give his life and strength to save the souls of poor abandoned Indians in the forests and jungles of Central America? Well, it has been my constant prayer for many years that the Lord might give me such a vocation, and it seems He has heard my prayer."

Father Gilbert J. Garraghan, S.J., in the third volume of his history *The Jesuits in the Middle United States,* gives a clear and precise description of the setting of Father Stanton's labors. Several attempts had been made to establish a mission center at Benque Viejo before Father Stanton's time. None succeeded on account of the difficulties involved. The place was about a hundred miles from Belize on the map. It took four days to reach it on horseback when the conditions for travel were favorable. When they were adverse, it might take two or three weeks. For the first four months in Benque, Father Stanton was alone. An assistant arrived after a primitive church and rectory had been erected. The presence of another priest at the post allowed Father Stanton to visit the outlying missions in his district, so that most of his time was spent without the company of a fellow Jesuit or of a white man of any kind. In one of his letters he writes: "Well, thank God, I got back safe and sound to Benque after thirty-two days in the bush. About three hundred and fifty miles I made on horseback." At another time, he says: "I have just returned to Benque, and, though somewhat sore in the bones, shall be all right in a couple of days. In trying to make one stretch, from a place called Orange Walk, where I had been for the First Friday, to the Cayo, a distance of about forty miles, I managed to get a late start and was caught by the night when about half way. I had been soaking wet all day, with nothing to eat but a cup of coffee and a biscuit in the morning, and had been in the saddle all day; and finally it was so dark, and still raining, and I was so tired at midnight that I had to dismount beside a little creek and throw myself on the ground just as I was, until I had light enough to see again. During the night my horse slipped his halter and made back toward his home, and morning found me alone, wet, tired, fasting from the morning before, with a pair of saddlebags weighing close on to fifty pounds, and about ten miles from any human being. There was nothing to do but to shoulder those bags and make through the mud for the Cayo. I arrived there in about five hours, and confess I could not have gone much further. As it was Sunday morning, I managed to get a change of clothes and succeeded in saying Mass; but for two days I was not able to mount a horse to get back home. I am better now and the aches are getting out of my bones. We are in the midst of the Rains now, and traveling through the forest trails at this time is not exactly a picnic. But it's God's work, and what more profitable can we be engaged in?"

Later in the same year, 1907, he tells in a letter of another of his forays after souls: "I have just returned safely from one of the dirtiest trips I have yet made. It was a visit to three different Indian towns hidden away in the deep bush. I have been away only a week, having made some hundred and sixty miles on horseback, the whole of it through dense jungle, where the midday sun scarcely penetrates, my poor beast plowing through sticky mud and tangled roots, usually sinking above his knees, whilst the rider, machete in hand, had to chop and cut through the mass of rank vegetation and hanging lianas that very often completely closed the so-called road, which is nothing but a narrow Indian trail."

These are a few specimens, selected at random, of the hardships described in Father Stanton's letters. What kind of people was he working for? Every now and then he tells us something about them. "The Indians and Peteneros are certainly the most miserable Indians I have yet had to deal with. They are far below the Filipinos in civilization, and so lazy that so long as there is a handful of corn in the house you could not get them to move a finger for love or money. . . . We are trying, however, to train the children, and in the evenings I take the boys in the last hour of school and teach them gardening. . . . These Indians of Yaalbaac, Chorro, and San Jose are all nominally Catholic, but are almost entirely ignorant of the teachings of the Church and full of all sorts of strange superstitions and pagan practices. They have their little bush church, where one finds the altar made of little saplings and sticks, sometimes covered over with clay and whitewashed. There are always a number of wooden crosses on it, dressed in rags and ribbons of various colors, and sometimes a picture of a saint, or colored advertisements, placards such as Schlitz's Beer, Reuter's Soap, or Hennessy's Brandy before which the poor creatures burn candles made from the wax of the wild bee, and incense which they get from the trees of the forest." Concubinage was common. As for their domestic habits, "In these Indian villages privacy is unknown, and usually the open woods as a sleeping place are preferable to the filthy cabins of the natives, filled with fleas and all sorts of vermin." The prevalent language was Maya: few spoke Spanish.

The last year of Father Stanton's life in the mission was especially heroic. He became the victim of a virulent cancer and at times suffered excruciating pain. The medical men in the colony could not make an accurate diagnosis, and Father Stanton took his attacks of pain as a kind of rheumatism not to be seriously considered. But the time came when his superiors concluded there was something worse than rheumatism present. A Jesuit returning to St. Louis took Father Stanton back with him at the beginning of January, 1910. The passage to the States was rough, and Father Stanton was in torture. He remained indomitable and cheerful, expecting a slight operation would restore him to his mission. About two months later he died in St. John's Hospital in St. Louis.

The mission which he founded in Benque Viejo is now flourishing. The place has seen great improvement spiritually and economically. Father Garraghan quotes a Belize pastor as saying that in the Benque Viejo district "the rate of concubinage had been brought down from eighty-five to twelve per cent."

CHAPTER 15

PERSECUTIONS

MARTYRDOM appears on the surface to be a quick and easy passport to heaven. The confessor Saint has to meet heroically the hourly challenges which a weak nature and an alluring world know so well how to make potent with a show of sweet reasonableness. The martyr has to meet but one sharp challenge, and it is all over. But it is to be doubted whether the matter is so simple. Martyrdom is a great grace which ordinarily implies a virtuous life of unusual excellence. A careless Christian is not likely to triumph in a supreme test of his love of God. It is not a mere question of dying voluntarily: one must die gladly with love in his heart for those who are killing him. St. Thomas More must have had his own opinion of Henry VIII and of the servile judges who perjured themselves to condemn him. But he expressed the hope that they would all meet again and be right merry in heaven in the end. St. John de Breboeuf must have experienced certain natural feelings uncomplimentary to the brutal savages who were exercising their ingenuity in choosing the most excruciating ways of making him suffer. The Saint had to overcome those feelings.

Because men and women, trying to be holy, do not shriek defiance at their tormentors, a large number of persons who seem to be intelligent have a curious notion that Christians who are persecuted and put to death for their religion are devoid of spirit, like cockroaches and cattle. When such persons hear that St. Ignatius prayed that his Order would never be without persecution, they read about the persecution of Jesuits, which is always going on somewhere, as if persecution was the natural element of a Jesuit and something too native for resentment. They never dream that a Jesuit might possibly be sensitive to injustice and calumny, to the discomforts of exile from his native land, to the robbery of his books and manuscripts, to aspersions on his character and motives, and even to imprisonment, massacre or public execution. A persecution of Jesuits is like a famine in China, a recurring item in small type on the inside pages of a newspaper, too common to be very tragic. The general impression seems to be that Jesuits and Chinese do not feel those things so acutely as the rest of the world.

There is one curious circumstance about the persecution of Jesuits which is absent in the misfortunes of the Chinese. Public opinion of the so-called enlightened kind may not be shocked at suffering in China, but it does not gloat over it. But, somehow or other, it almost invariably happens that, when Jesuits are the victims of violent treatment, public opinion is maneuvered into the position of regarding their hard case with a certain amount of actual approval. Thus, when more than a hundred peaceful Jesuits were slaughtered in the recent civil war in Spain, most of the agencies of public opinion in the United States and England were on the side of their murderers. The great newspapers, the best foreign correspondents, the organizations dedicated to culture and humanity, the prominent ministers and rabbis, and even some of the more cultured Catholics, were definitely in favor of a government which slew, or allowed to be slain, over a thousand priests and nuns with barbaric ferocity. All these very enlightened people can, no doubt, explain their philosophic resignation to the persecution of Jesuits on what seem to them to be noble and exalted grounds. It has always been so. A Jesuit in America suffers keenly in his sympathies with his brothers who are kicked about and trampled to death in Spain or some other country; but the thing he feels most is the cruel and callous attitude of public opinion which clothes itself in the self-conscious virtue of a wise benevolence and a lofty idealism.

During those atrocious Spanish days, which ushered in the civil war and exiled the Jesuits after burning their houses, there was one honest, pure-souled, keen-eyed molder of public opinion who never allowed himself to be caught up and carried along by the manufactured hysterics of a radical coterie. That was Gilbert Keith Chesterton. He loved liberty and humanity as ardently as any radical. But his devotion to liberty, democracy, and humanity was more intelligent and enlightened than that of the common species of radical which seems to be able to create prevalent opinion. Chesterton wrote a poem on the Jesuits which I am going to quote if for no other reason than to give the reader some idea of the natural reflection of a Jesuit when he or his associates are going through one of their recurring persecutions.

The poem is filled with historical allusions which may be obscure to a reader not familiar with the history of the Jesuits. For that reason I am going, by way of introduction, to give a brief explanation, in the order in which they occur, of the references the poet had in mind.

1. In China Fathers Ricci and Schall and their fellow Jesuits in the sixteenth and seventeenth centuries obtained mandarin rank and a foothold for Catholic missions by their mathematical and astronomical learning and the building of observatories.

2. In Paraguay the early Jesuit missionaries won difficult access to the savage aborigines by the use of musical instruments and the teaching of hymns. From this beginning they not only Christianized the natives but organized them into an actual Utopia. It is generally conceded that, as a social experiment, this achievement has been the most successful among the many attempts to establish a paradise on earth with the poor material of our fallen human nature. R. B. Cunninghame Graham, in *A Vanished Arcadia,* gives an interesting picture of the happy commonwealth. But the paradise was ruthlessly invaded and completely stamped out under the iron-shod hoofs of greed and brutality.

3. There were not wanting in the early colonial history of this country and other countries on the western hemisphere accusations against the Jesuit missionaries that they identified themselves with the Indians to the extent of being equally guilty with them of all the outrages perpetrated by the savages. The only good Indian was a dead Indian: the Jesuits were the enemies of humanity simply by consorting with the living kind.

4. The principles of democracy, first broached in the middle ages, were taught by some of the Jesuit philosophers and theologians before democratic forms of government in the modern sense had come into existence.

5. Contrary to the oft-repeated view that Jesuits attach themselves to the stronger political party, they have been, when religion and conscience dictated, the last defenders of hopeless causes.

6. The Jesuit doctrine on salvation, like all Catholic doctrine, holds out hope for the most hardened and degenerate sinners. Because they have been patient, within the strict limits of religion and morality, with the weaknesses of human nature, the Jesuits have been accused of teaching lax morality by those who concede that the private life of a Jesuit conforms to high moral standards. The obvious contradiction seems to have no weight.

7. Bacon wrote in his *Advancement of Learning:* "Education: which excellent part of ancient discipline hath been in some sort revived of late times by the colleges of the Jesuits; of whom, although in regard to their superstition I may say, 'Quo meliores, eo deteriores' (The better they are, the worse it is), yet in regard of this, and some other points concerning human learning and moral matters, I may say, as Agesilaus said to his enemy Pharnabazus, 'Talis quum sis, utinam noster esses' (Since you are so good, would you were on our side)." Jesuits may be learned and competent teachers, but they teach ignorance, superstition, and obscurantism!

8. Jesuits, whose only purpose in becoming Jesuits was to re-
tire from the selfish complications of secular life to leave themselves free to cultivate love of God and their neighbor, have
always been characterized by their enemies as self-seekers,
mischief-makers, fomenters of dissension, and troublesome
plotters in the state.

With these annotations, the reader may increase his pleasure
in the poem. Even without any tiresome explanations, the
poem gives a noble expression to honest human feeling which
no lover of poetry can miss. That it should be Chesterton who
did this, is all the more remarkable because, as far as I know,
no Jesuit has ever been mentioned as being among his intimate
Catholic friends.

TO THE JESUITS

By G. K. Chesterton
(Spain 1936)

Flower-wreathed with all unfading calumnies,
Scarlet and splendid with eternal slander,
How should you hope, where'er the world may wander,
To lose the long laudation of its lies.

The yellow gods of sunrise saw arise
Your titled towers that housed the moons and suns,
The red suns of the sunset, not with guns
But with guitars, you ambushed for surprise.

You bade the Red Man rise like the Red Clay
Of God's great Adam in his human right,
Till trailed the snake of trade, our own time's blight,
And Man lost Paradise in Paraguay.

You, when wild sects tortured and mocked each other,
Saw truth in the wild tribes that tortured you;
Slurred for not slurring all who slurred or slew,
Blamed that your murderer was too much your brother.

You hailed before its dawn Democracy,
Which in its death bays you with demagogues:
You dared strong kings that hunted you with dogs
To hide some hunted king in trench or tree.

When Calvin's Christ, made Antichrist, had caught
Even the elect and all men's hearts were hardened,
You were called profligates because you pardoned,
And tools of ignorance because you taught.

All that warped world your charity could heal,
And the world's charity was not for you;
How should you hope deliverance in things new,
In this last chance twist of the world's wheel?

One, while that wheel as a vast top is twirled
With every age, realm, riot, pomp, or pact,
Thrown down in thunder like a cataract,
Said "Fear not; I have overthrown the world."

It would be leaving a false impression to lead anyone to
infer that Jesuits have what is called a persecution complex
and pose as martyrs because of their vicissitudes. If a Jesuit has
the spirit of his Society and sees in persecution an opportunity
of exercising his love of God and imitating his Divine Master,
he will take persecutions in his stride, with a wounded sense
of justice perhaps, but without cowering or self-pity. Jesuits
who are having a hard time anywhere are likely to be envied
by their brethren who have more peaceful berths. Volunteers
for dangerous posts are never lacking. If a Jesuit is not always
confident of finding cooperation and understanding in pleading and working for a worthy cause, he considers himself not
worse off than most Catholic priests and most philanthropic
reformers. But he so often discovers goodness and fairness in
unlikely quarters that he is ready to meet every stranger on a

friendly basis and to make large allowance for differences of training and environment. And he can always count on devoted friends. The Society has been abundantly blessed with them in its darkest hours.

CHAPTER 16

WHY PERSECUTIONS?

"IT IS hard," says Hazlitt, "to praise those who are despised by others. He is little short of a hero who persists in thinking well of a friend who has become a butt of slander and a byword." As Newman wrote in defending his reputation after he had been traduced up and down the country for twenty years, people naturally conclude that there must be something in accusations so widespread and enduring; that it is more likely, "where much is imputed something must be true, and it is more likely that one should be to blame than that many should be mistaken in blaming him." Newman saw the futility of replying seriatim to the charges against his sincerity and honesty: his only effective course was to lay bare his inner life from childhood on and to explain the motives, reasons, and circumstances attending every step on his road to Rome. The picture which Newman gave of his interior life stilled forever the campaign of calumny. That is the only way the Society of Jesus can hope to meet slander. I have accordingly in these pages attempted to give some notion of the interior spirit of the Society, the spirit which should inform and dominate the life of every Jesuit, rather than to assume the gigantic and useless task of answering every count in an endless bill of particulars.

I am far from denying that Jesuits have made mistakes and incurred just blame; and their enemies have made the most of such instances. It would be foolish to claim inerrancy for the Society, or prudence, discretion, and the possession of every virtue for all its members. In a world of puzzling crosscurrents, it is not easy at times, even with the best intentions, to choose the practical course which is the wisest. It would be easy to play safe and do nothing; but playing safe, in the sense of holding aloof when religion and the salvation of souls are at stake, was not the idea of St. Ignatius. Moreover, making due allowance for divine grace and the guidance of the Church, it has to be kept in mind that the Society has to operate through the natural character, disposition, and individual traits of its members. They are men in a world of men. They do not divest themselves of human nature when they become Jesuits, nor does the Society wish them to. It expects them to discipline their nature to a point where it can be employed as a useful instrument in giving greater glory to God. They must satisfy the requirement of a certain minimum of fitness and promise, or the Society will reject them. But, over and above that minimum, no limits, except those of divine grace, are set, and generous and valorous souls will yield themselves unreservedly to the molding processes of a Society that knows how to make saints.

Generosity and valor are not commonplace virtues. It is a matter for each Jesuit to determine for himself just how far he will go beyond the minimum in responding to the gentle urgence of the Society toward a wholehearted surrender to his vocation. His reluctance will be the measure of his failure as an exemplary Jesuit and of the degree in which he falls short of what the Society has a right to expect of him. Without going to the extreme of leaving the Society, or being dismissed from it, he can be in minor ways a troublesome member and can supply a certain amount of comfort to those who take delight in discovering flaws in Jesuits. After all, human nature does not take kindly to the heroic mold. All I wish to say is that the ideal of the Society, its Constitution, its rules, its spirituality, its history and tradition, its system of checks, are all designed to create a type of man altogether different from that so often described in unfriendly history. I dare say the Society can compare favorably with any large secular organization of noble ideals and principles that has lasted four hundred years. It is only fair that any organized group should be judged by its principles and not by contrary instances, especially if the line of illustrious instances has from first to last preserved that continuity of tone and general character impressed upon it by its founder.

Although good men have sometimes ranged themselves against the Society, it would be willing, I think, to be judged by the character of the general run of its enemies.

Opposition to the Jesuits may be summarized under a few headings:

1. They have to contend with that hostile tone of worldly society which all clergymen have to face. As Newman pointed out in the sermon which got Charles Kingsley into trouble, the man of the world has an instinctive dislike for priests and all ministers of religion. The man of the world will deny this, but I do not see how he can escape the cold and penetrating analysis of that sermon. What are called red-blooded, manly men have a secret, if not open, contempt for a class of persons who do not fight back, and they harbor the suspicion that such persons employ cunning and underhand means to attain their ends. "Still stronger," continues Newman, "is this delusion on the part of the world, when the event justifies the confidence of religious men. The truest wisdom is to stand still and trust in God, and to the world it is also the strongest evidence of craft. God fights for those who do not fight for themselves; such is the great truth, such is the gracious rule, which is declared and exemplified in the Gospel: 'Dearly beloved, avenge not yourselves,' says St. Paul, 'but rather give place unto wrath, for it is written, Vengeance is Mine, I will repay, saith the Lord.' Do nothing, and you have done everything. The less you do, the more God will do for you. The more you submit to the violence of the world, the more powerfully will He rise against the world, Who is irresistible. The less you ward off the world's blows from you, the more heavy will be His blows

upon the world, if not in your cause, at least in His own. When, then, the world at length becomes sensible that it is faring ill, and receiving more harm than it inflicts, yet is unwilling to humble itself under the mighty hand of God, what is left but to attribute its failure to the power of those who seem to be weak? that is, to their craft, who pretend to be weak when really they are strong."

2. Exaggerated nationalism is a fertile source of hostility. The doctrine of universality which its divine Founder entrusted to His Church when He bade His Apostles and disciples to teach the whole world, not this nation or that to the exclusion of any other, is always unsatisfactory to the national pride which wants nothing in common with other countries and does not easily brook interference, even in spiritual matters, from abroad. The Jesuits are vowed to the defense of the papacy. They are ultramontane. Whenever nationalism runs wild, as it so often has done in the past and continues to do, the Society of Jesus is among the first to feel its anger.

3. The Protestant tradition, "to be a true Protestant is but to hate the Pope," accounts, of course, for much calumny in non-Catholic countries.

4. Enemies of religion everywhere — anticlericals, communists, secret societies — do the Jesuits the honor of choosing them for special opprobrium.

5. In the Catholic Church, good men of virtuous life have sometimes felt obliged to oppose the Society. In a world where the best of men do not always see eye to eye even in a holy cause, these collisions cannot properly be alleged as evidence against the moral and spiritual character of the Jesuit Order. The laborers in the vineyard are numerous, and it is not at all strange that they should at times get in one another's way. Their very zeal will often start and lend fuel to a quarrel. These domestic feuds are in a different class from the onslaughts of the common enemy outside the vineyard. Whenever the Society is expelled from any portion of the vineyard,

I think it will be found that the loudest cheers come from outside the Church. If some zealous colaborers in the vineyard can bear its expulsion with cheerful resignation, no thoughtful critic will conclude that the Society was fundamentally unsound.

If I have omitted from this list any notable cause of enmity toward the Society, the omission has not been intentional. The list could be longer. It might contain, for instance, some mention of the widespread and persistent belief that Jesuits are the possessors of fabulous wealth, one of the secrets of their power. Alas, if this belief were well-founded, there would be fewer heartaches and sleepless nights for the weary men who are responsible for making ends meet in many a good work. Contrary to quite common opinion, no central fund exists anywhere in the Society for financing its missions and colleges. Each unit has to get along on its own resources, and for most, if not for all the units, the struggle for existence seldom reaches the haven of a comfortable security. There are in this country a half-dozen private universities whose combined endowment approaches closely to half a billion, over and above their costly buildings and equipment. Such institutions must look down on Jesuits as in the pauper class. It is an interesting fact for all believers of Jesuit opulence to mull over, that some Jesuit schools have been excluded by standardizing agencies from their accredited list principally on account of their poverty.

If there are in other countries Jesuit schools rolling in wealth, I have not heard of them. Preying governments, that every decade or so swoop down on them hopefully, are always disappointed with the amount of loot. As for the rich patrons, whom the wily Jesuit in the Macaulay tradition had the art of winning over for his own purposes, I am inclined to believe that the art, if the Jesuits ever possessed it, has long since passed into other hands and is employed in causes less religious and spiritual than those to which a Jesuit is devoted.

CHAPTER 17

THE SUPPRESSION

WHEN the Jesuits were suppressed in 1773, 23,000 men were cut loose from their moorings and most of them sent adrift without provisions, each to fend for himself, in a world which they had forsaken and where they were as strangers from another planet. They knew and felt keenly that they were victims of lying intrigues and powerful political cabals. Pombal, de Choiseul, Pompadour — God rest their souls! If any critic of the Society thinks he ought to put them in his shrine of noble public benefactors for private devotion, he can have them.

Among those 23,000, many were old and infirm men who were lost and bewildered at finding themselves in their declining years and failing health flung into the streets without a home. Those who were dragged to prison dungeons were saved, at least, from the need of taking thought for the morrow. The young, the middle aged, and the robust, their tendrils rudely torn from their ancient walls, probably found eventually some sort of frame for a patterned life. The scholars, deprived of their manuscripts and books, the missioners in remote lands, shipped back to Europe like cattle after long years of absence, who can tell, and when shall we know, what loneliness, what sense of defeat, what melancholy memories were the thronging ghosts of their last days! Is it too much to say that the suppression of the Society of Jesus was, from a human point of view, one of the great tragedies of history with few parallels in poignancy and magnitude?

And yet literature, which finds its inspiration in great tragedy, seems to have passed it over. Where are the memoirs, the journals, the ruck of books and pamphlets which tragedy of world-wide dimensions usually leaves in its wake? It is true, the triumphant enemies of the Society licked their chops in various productions; but these were too coarse and violent to be classed as literature, like the cries of a glutted mob after an execution. Literature at its best must have dignity, and the dignity of patient sorrow is the dignity which it finds noblest in a world like ours. Why did not the stricken Jesuits speak out? They were not inarticulate: as a body they were the most articulate men of the time. They were not unlettered Acadians, who, like the poor and unlettered of every age, had to bear injustice and tyranny with pathetic endurance. As a Jesuit, I can enter into their feelings and sympathize with them; and, in doing so, I think all true hearts, alive to wrongs and sufferings, will go along with me. But I cannot readily recall any Jesuit apology or memoir published at the time commemorating and in some way satisfying justifiable curiosity about a great historical episode and about the burden of grief it brought upon the members of a great Society. A few *disjecta membra* rise to the surface of history after the wreck — one of the suppressed Society became the first Archbishop of Baltimore; some of them formed an association in France, called "Fathers of the Faith," and another in Belgium, "Fathers of the Sacred Heart"; 23 perished in the French Revolution; small groups continued to function in Prussia and Russia where the Papal Brief of Suppression was not promulgated — not much more is heard of those 23,000. They simply disappeared like snow on moving waters. An awful silence seemed to settle down upon them forever.

Two cruel alternatives faced them. If they spoke out, they would be accused of disobedience and rebellion: if they kept still, they would be derided as wrongdoers suddenly exposed and scuttling for cover. The logic of the situation actually con-

demned them to silence. If they were thrown to the wolves to
save what they were sworn to defend at any cost, they could
not well repine. As spiritually trained men with a supernatural
philosophy of life, they accepted their fate as the will of God.
But it was a trial worse than death. They had to continue living after their saint-making mother was slain and her name
made a by-word in the halls and highways of the world.

St. Ignatius said that it would take him not more than a
quarter of an hour to reconcile himself cheerfully to the ex-
tinction of his Society. There are, not unlikely, some easy-chair
saints who will find fault with him for taking so long. It is
remarkable how inhuman the critics of the saints sometimes
are. This gentry will be shocked to learn that one, at least, of
the disbanded Jesuits, while submitting to authority, never
succeeded in achieving the heroism of cheerfulness over its
decision. He did not "publish his wistfulness abroad"; his
sorrow was his own secret; and, being a poet, he put it into a
poem which was found among his papers after his active pen
had been laid aside forever. It is a truly noble poem, with the
added interest of affording us a glimpse of what was going on
in the deep recesses of souls doomed to silence in a tragic hour.
In submitting quietly to the decree of Providence, they could
not help reflecting bitterly on the chicanery and calumnies of
crooked politicians and corrupt courts and their subservient
press, the grafting petty officials, the open and avowed assailants
of Christianity who rejoiced in their fall. Diderot was jubilant:
but we hear of no saint joining in his mirth. St. Alphonsus
Liguori showed his grief and made a memorable prophecy:
"I do not fear to say, in spite of all appearances to the contrary,
that even though there were but one Jesuit left in the world,
that last surviving member will suffice to restore the Society."

The author of the following poem did not live to see the
Society restored; but his poem inclines us to believe that, if he
were the last Jesuit of St. Alphonsus' prediction, he would go
far toward fulfilling it. Michael Denis was born in Bavaria in

1729 and entered the Society of Jesus in Vienna when he was eighteen. He was teaching in the "Theresianum," a famous college of the Jesuits in Vienna, when the suppression came, and fared better than many of his brothers in the disaster by retaining his post of professor, and by his appointment some years later as librarian of the Imperial Library in Vienna. The *Catholic Encyclopedia* devotes a column to him; the notice in the *Britannica* is briefer. Besides attaining fame as a bibliographer, he was not only a noted poet himself but also the founder of a German school of poetry and the German translator of Ossian's poems. The Nagl-Zeidler-Castle *History of Literature* contains an account of him and his school. It is surmised that the poem we reproduce was written in the early nineties of the eighteenth century while the French Revolution was spreading dismay over the civilized world. Two alternative titles have been given it, *The Fate of the Society of Jesus,* or *To My Suppressed Society*. It reads like King Arthur's lament over the lost glory of Camelot.

I venture to offer a prose version in English — wholly lacking the Latin neatness of the original distichs — which may convey some idea of their passionate feeling, a quality seldom possessed by the academic pentameters of modern classical poets writing Latin verse. For the convenience of the reader the two versions follow on opposite pages.

They are nearly all gone — the men of that goodly company who of old counted me one of them, such as I was, till Hell with crafty art equipped all its human hirelings to destroy us.

Prostitute tongues, vitriolic pens, sham panic, spite, greed, all hemmed us in, a yelping circle of assault, while we fought a lone fight unaided.

What mattered that we had moulded the minds of the young to culture and taught them the ways of virtue;

had produced so many illustrious men that the books heralding their deathless fame are too numerous to reckon;

had sown the seed of God's law in city and town and farm; watched by day and by night with equal concern beside the state-beds of dying kings and the pallets of the poor; dyed with our sweat and our blood every region east and west under the sun so that there was nowhere a spot on the face of the earth too remote to be filled with the fruits of our service for Christ and His holy religion!

All this counted for nothing.

We were ejected from our homes, dispersed, and, contrary to our desires, absolved from our allegiance of brotherhood.

There was no recourse in law, no tribunal with benefit of trial and jury.

Alas, for the irresistible power of sinister forces when they agree in a malignant purpose!

And alas, for the midnight darkness that can descend upon the human heart!

Did you fondly hope, O Europe, that the golden age would return once you had made an end of us?

What befoolment! Lift your eyes, look anywhere at all, see what the world has come to!

You behold rebel populace and panic-striken ruler at each other's throat; churches desecrated, altars reeking with the blood of sacrilege, walls crumbling in ruin and desolation.

You see in the cities forsaken homes and in the countryside tenantless farms, scarce anywhere an asylum for your wretched refugees.

Pauca sodalitii superant jam membra beati
  Cujus ego quondam pars quotacumque fui;
Cujus in excidium sollers armavit Avernus
  Quidquid ei toto militat orbe mali.
Venales pretio linguae, mordacia scripta,
  Conficti metus, livor, opumque sitis
Agmine nos facto circumfremuere, nec usquam
  Cura laborantes ulla levare fuit.
Nil juvat ingenuis teneram formasse juventam
  Artibus, et mores edocuisse bonos;
Tot claros genuisse viros, quos nescia mortis
  Innumeris loquitur fama voluminibus;
Semina divinae legis sparsisse per urbes,
  Oppida et agrestis fumida tecta casae;
Pulvillis regum morientum inopumque grabatis
  Advigilasse pari nocte dieque fide;
Tinxisse extremas sudore et sanguine terras,
  Quas oriens Phoebus lustrat et occiduus,
Ut regio nusquam nostri non plena laboris
  Pro Christo et sancta religione foret.
Nil juvat. Exigimur laribus, disjungimur, atque
  Fraterno inviti solvimur officio.
Non tamen ulla data est culpatis curia, nulla est
  Legitimo nobis causa peracta foro.
Proh! tantum potuit vis conjurata malorum,
  Tantum hominum caecae pectora noctis habent!
Scilicet aurea saecla tibi reditura putabas,
  Europa, a nostri clade sodalitii?
Credula! tolle oculos, partem circumfer in omnem,
  Et quae sit facies rerum hodierna vide.
Aspicis infestos populos, agitataque regna,
  Alterum in alterius proruere exitium;
Templa profanata et pollutas caedibus aras
  Undique et horrendo diruta tecta situ;
Cive domos vacuas desertaque rura colono,
  Perfugium miseris vix super exulibus.

Impiety lifts its insolent front to the heavens, laws are trampled underfoot, public confidence destroyed, justice and decency exiled.

Your youths, recklessly defying all restraint, perish in their prime.

I am not in the vindictive mood to call down vengeance nor do I wish to see in these calamities the aftermath of our ashes.

There is, it is true, a current belief that this doom might have been averted, or, at least, been less sweeping had we continued in the field.

We would perhaps have sealed a glorious cause with our blood or helped to restore something like sanity to the public mind.

Perhaps. As for me, I do not share in this sublime confidence. I see in events the will of God and bow down before it.

I am not denied the poor privilege of visiting the graves of my brothers, and in spirit clasping to my heart the few survivors scattered over the globe, and when this weary life is done, may the last day reunite us forever!

Till then I will carry down with me to my grave an unfailing hope. It is this: That posterity, unswayed by hate or favor, will weigh the deeds of my Society and pronounce the verdict:

"A fellowship like this never flourished of old, and future ages, strive as they may, shall not see its like again."

*　　*　　*

Father Denis died in 1800, apparently less hopeful of the Society's rebirth than St. Alphonsus. His feeling that the ultimate had happened will excuse any excess of fervor noticeable in the closing lines; that and his affectionate attachment to the Society. Father Bernhard Duhr, S.J., in his *History of the German Jesuits,* has some interesting pages about Father Denis and his life in the Society. He was an upright religious man keenly sensitive to the disgrace of his Order and submitting without loud complaints. If he sought relief privately by expressing his *saeva indignatio* in distichs for his own perusal, who will condemn him?

Insultat coelo impietas; reverentia legum
  Nulla; fides cessit; fasque pudorque procul.
Omne ruit temere fraenum indignata juventus
  Et florem aetatis deterit ante diem.
Non ego sum Nemesim qui coelo devocet, aut qui
  Cuncta haec de nostro funere nata velit.
Sunt tamen averti, aut minui, potuisse ruinam,
  Qui nostro incolumi corpore stante putent.
Signassemus enim praeclaram sanguine causam
  Aut populis nostra mens rediisset ope.
Haec alii. Mihi non tanta est fiducia nostri.
  Supremi veneror Numinis arbitrium.
Quodque licet tumulos obeo, sparsasque per orbem
  Complector fratrum pectore reliquias,
Queis ubi summa dies jam fessum junxerit aevo.
  Haec erit ad tumulum spes mihi fida comes:
Posteritas quae non odio nec amore feretur
  Pensabitque mei gesta sodalitii,
"Coetum talem hominum," dicet, "nec prisca tulere
  Nec, conata licet, saecla futura ferent."

*   *   *

CHAPTER 18

INDIAN GIVING AND THE
SHOE-HORN TRICK

WHENEVER a gift is conferred with a large generous gesture and afterwards withdrawn by the giver, it is said to be an Indian gift. Why this mean practice should be thus associated with Indians, I do not know. Most early accounts of the aborigines, in North America, at least, represent them as possessing noble natural traits.

The Jesuits have been the doubtful beneficiaries of munificent Indian giving in their time, especially of late. The new style of history writing, called scientific, boasts of being objective, taking nothing for granted, rejecting secondhand sources, consulting original documents, being strictly on guard against popular and traditional concepts, and unswayed by popular and personal prejudices. Writers who have approached the Society of Jesus in this frame of mind have been rather astonished at the number of good points they discover in it. Being honest men, they give credit where credit is due, regardless of consequences. The simple Jesuit reads the new biography or history, turning page after page eagerly with a purring contentment, and saying to himself, "Here at last we are getting something like our due from a world that has been always unfair to us; what a refreshing treat it is to behold the snow-white form of Truth lifting her shining countenance above the serried phalanxes of darkness!"

Fond man! Let him hug contentment for a while. It will be rudely torn from his arms in the last paragraph, or the last page, or the last chapter. There it will be insinuated by the honest and industrious and patient author that, while it is quite true the Society is a remarkable organization with a remarkable history and with many examples of virtue and heroism, too often maligned and treated with great injustice, and not nearly so bad as popular opinion holds, still history, impartial history, cannot give it a clean bill. It has been great and good in its own way; but its way was bad. Its principles were faulty. It wasted heroic efforts in the pursuit of wrong ideals.

When discussion shifts its ground from matters of fact to a philosophy of life in these modern days, anything at all can be made to appear plausible. These are days of no fixed principles in morals and religion outside of Catholic circles. Any modern writer claims the right of drawing up his own code of morals and religion; and, if the Society of Jesus does not conform to that private code, he feels justified in declaring in all good faith and without any consciousness of bias, that the Society is and has been immoral and un-Christian. The instruments for discovering moral and religious truths, unlike those for the discovery of physical truths, have not been multiplied and improved in the past hundred years. But modern writers proceed blithely on the assumption that they have been somehow equipped more effectively for discovery in morals and religion than men have been at any time in the past two thousand years. It requires no boldness or effrontery whatever for any penny-a-liner or ambitious university instructor to contradict openly the moral judgments of a hundred generations of thoughtful students of human nature.

A nice example of Indian giving was afforded some years ago by that popular writer, René Fülöp-Miller, in his book, *The Power and Secret of the Jesuits*. The author, while disclaiming the dignity of a professional historian, went to considerable pains to compose what he wished to be an objective and impartial account of the Society. He consulted everybody, the enemies of the Society as well as its friends; and, in the manner of an able journalist at his best, tries to hold the balance even and tell an interesting story. As the title of his book suggests, he is not averse to the spectacular wherever he finds it; but, for a man of the world writing for men of the world, with little or no religious experience to help him, he is like Doctor Johnson's dog, performing on its hind legs, and does very well. As such histories go, his is remarkably favorable to the Jesuits — until nearly the end. It would seem he became conscious that he had praised them more than he had intended or expected.

This would never do. He looked the world over for some oracular and impressive verdict which would shatter the palace of music he had built. Needless to say, he found what he sought. It was not a great theologian, not a great saint, nor a serious student of Christianity, nor even a sane and practical man of the world, who supplied him with the corrosive agent he required. He chose a Russian, with that peculiarly Russian ideology so strange and chaotic to Western civilization, a popular novelist of wild genius and bohemian habits, whose principal recreation was gambling, to pronounce the final verdict on the Jesuits. And that verdict was, that the Jesuits were not spiritual enough and had done infinite harm to the mission of Christ by lowering its aim and making it too easy for the cowardly spirit of man. Thus Pascal and Mère Angelique got two more recruits, Dostoievsky and Fülöp-Miller. Somehow they do not look quite at home in Port Royal.

Macaulay's famous digression on the Jesuits in his *History of England* is undoubtedly the most flagrant instance of Indian giving in human annals. No partisan of the Jesuits at his peak of enthusiasm has ever pronounced such an eloquent eulogy of the Order. Macaulay snatches the reader away in a veritable whirlwind of laudatory rhetoric and carries him along at tremendous speed for three hundred years from the birth of the Order to modern times until the reader is breathless with awe and admiration. And then suddenly all the magnificent rhetoric goes into reverse and travels backwards with equal speed like a freak motor car in some nightmare of the cinema. At the end nothing is left of the poor Jesuits; not a rag of respectability.

It is in this second part of the digression that Macaulay employs the shoe-horn trick. Mr. Belloc has invented the phrase and I shall let him describe it. "Mr. Wells falls into the common trick or error (I prefer to call it an error rather than a trick in this case, for he is a man, though limited, sincere) which I will baptize the 'shoe-horn,' and with which I became wonderfully well acquainted at Oxford. It consists in putting a thing as a possibility on one page, as a probability on a later page, and on a still later page as a certitude."

Macaulay begins his striking antithesis with a definite and positive statement of what he takes to be a fact. "But with the admirable energy, disinterestedness, and self-devotion which were characteristic of the Society, great vices were mingled." After pages of inspired panegyric, this drops like a bombshell with all the studied effect that Macaulay loved. And then begins the long indictment. One would expect it to start out with some clause running like this: "It has been proved beyond the shadow of a doubt"; or, one like this: "The most serious and nonpartisan historians all agree that." How does it actually run? Here it is: "It was alleged, and not without foundation." If the shoe does not fit the Jesuit foot, let us have the shoe-horn: we will get it on; just wait! There is no doubt about the thing having been alleged, and even with some foundation. There is no crime in the calendar that cannot be alleged with some foundation against the most innocent man in the world. "Alleged" is a useful and safe word for an author who does not want to be contradicted.

"It was alleged, and not without foundation" that the Jesuits were:

1. Merciless liars;

2. Utterly unscrupulous in promoting their own interests at the expense of the Catholic Church.

The second clause introduces new crimes with the same formula: *"It was alleged* that":

1. The Jesuits were active agents in the most atrocious plots in history;

2. They were timeservers;

3. They were the enemies of existing governments;

4. Their famed exploits were, "in the judgment of *many* illustrious members of the Church," specious and theatrical.

Here, it will be observed, another shoe-horn has been brought into use. The unsuspecting reader will not pause to ask himself who these illustrious members of the Church were. Were they saints? Were they the supreme authorities in the Church? And then we have another shoe-horn: *"It was reported"* that the Jesuits converted heathens by concealing unpleasant Christian doctrines and allowing them to conform outwardly to idol worship. The shoe has to be forced on; let us have another shoe-horn: "Nor was it only in heathen countries that such arts *were said* to be practised":

1. They competed with Dominicans and Franciscans in trying to draw penitents to their confessionals by lowering the standards of morality.

2. In their officially approved textbooks for the guidance of confessors, they found ways of excusing robbery, adultery, duelling, assassination, and perjury.

Now the shoe is on. Away with the shoe-horns. And Macaulay exults: "In truth, if society continued to hold together, if life and property enjoyed any security, it was because common sense and common humanity restrained men from doing what the Order of Jesus assured them they might with a safe conscience do. So strangely *were good and evil intermixed* in the character of these celebrated brethren." It is no longer an allegation; nor an allegation, not without foundation; nor the opinion of some illustrious members of the Church; nor hearsay; nor a report; but a fact.

If it was said that Jesuit handbooks of morality taught that murder and perjury might be practised without violating the moral laws, why, in the name of anything at all, did he not consult one of those handbooks in the nearest library to verify what surely must seem to be a most extraordinary charge against a large body of intelligent and religious men operating under the approval of a Church that has held society together better than any institution in the knowledge even of a Macaulay?

About the time Macaulay was writing his sketch of the Jesuits, Newman was delivering a course of lectures in the Corn Exchange at Birmingham. In one of those lectures, he elucidated the Macaulay-mind, which was, of course, the popular mind. Speaking of the popular prejudice against Catholics in England, he said, "the more I think of it, the more intimately does this prejudice seem to me to corrupt the soul, even beyond those sins which are commonly called deadly, as the various forms of impurity or pride. And why? because, I repeat it, it argues so astonishing a want of mere natural charity or love of our kind. It is piercing enough to think what little faith there is in the country; but it is heartrending to witness so utter a deficiency in a mere natural virtue. Oh, is it possible that so many, many men, and women too, good and kind otherwise, should take such delight in being quite sure that millions of men have the sign and seal of the Evil One upon them! Oh, is it conceivable that they can be considerate in all matters of this life, friendly in social intercourse, indulgent to the wayward, charitable to the poor and outcast, merciful towards criminals, nay, kind towards the inferior creation, toward their cows, and horses, and swine; yet, as regards us, who bear the same form, speak the same tongue, breathe the same air, and walk the same streets, ruthless, relentless, believing ill of us, and wishing to believe it! I repeat, they wish us to be what they believe us to be; what a portentous fact! They delight to look at us, and to believe we are the veriest reptiles and vermin which belied the human form divine. It is a dear thought which they cannot bear to lose. True, it may have been taught them from their youth, they may never have had the means to unlearn it — that is not the point; they have never *wished* better things of us, they have never *hoped* better things. They are tenacious of what they believe, they are impatient of being argued with, they are angry at being contradicted, they are disappointed when a point is cleared up; they had rather that *we* should be guilty than *they* mistaken; they have no wish at all we should not be blaspheming hypocrites, stupid idolaters, loathsome profligates, unprincipled rogues and bloodthirsty demons."

With a public like that, Macaulay's little shoe-horn trick was sure to succeed. And I am not sure that it is not still working with uncounted multitudes. I would like to believe that most intelligent and educated people today take Macaulay's Jesuit for the caricature it is. But I would not like to put the matter to a test.

It would be inaccurate and unjust to leave the impression that all non-Catholic writers on the Society have been made incompetent by the bias of an ineradicable tradition. The Reverend Robert Harvey, a clergyman in the United Church of Canada, has written a remarkably just and sympathetic life of Ignatius Loyola. It is so filled with understanding that it would be unreasonable to expect many like it from similar sources. Henry Dwight Sedgwick's *Life of Ignatius Loyola* and the Reverend Paul Van Dyke's *Ignatius Loyola* strive honestly after fairness. The most a Jesuit can look for, as a rule, from writers to whom, on account of their training and settled points of view, Catholic institutions are obscure and difficult subjects, is a genuine and sincere eagerness to be conscious of, and make allowance for, their own limitations.

An example of this attitude is to be found in a paragraph of Mr. Sedgwick's *Ignatius Loyola,* which I have quoted in the first chapter of this book. But it takes more than a smart journalist, or a mere mouthpiece of popular passions to write like Mr. Sedgwick. It calls for a magnanimous man so to regard an ancestral hobgoblin. Stevenson could do it, and, in his later years, Sir Walter Scott. In this respect, Carlyle and Emerson and Macaulay were hopelessly provincial to the end.

CHAPTER 19

THE EMBITTERED EX-JESUIT

THE ex-Jesuit, who exploits his experience in the Society by writing a book of "exposures," has been a fairly constant phenomenon from the earliest days of the Society. Usually the book stirs a momentary flurry in the reading world because it appeals to idle curiosity and hints at savory scandals. As far as I can recall, no such book has ever acquired the respectable standing of a solid contribution to history. Usually its obviously splenetic vein rules it out of court as disinterested testimony.

Among those who wish to discredit the Society, the ex-Jesuit enjoys exceptional advantages. He has passed some of the best years of his life in the bosom of the family and should be familiar with those domestic infelicities which arise in the secure privacy of every family and which the laws of honor and good taste require its members to conceal. He gives a keyhole view, and justifies himself by professions of sincerity and a benevolent desire to help the world at large.

It is a rather curious fact that the embittered ex-Jesuit may be sincere and consciously truthful, and yet may give a distorted and utterly false view of the Society. This apparent contradiction calls for explanation.

The only motive that can be called rational for entering the Society is a supernatural motive. The one and single purpose of the Society is to afford facilities for growing in spiritual perfection. It impresses this purpose upon every aspirant for membership. The youth who becomes a Jesuit for any other reason than that of securing his eternal salvation, advancing in perfection, and inducing others to take thought for their souls, is committed at the very start to a life of cross-purposes and disappointments. If he embraces the life of the Society to satisfy intellectual ambition, or acquire social prestige, or enjoy economic security, and to have his own way in pursuing these or any other private ends of his own, he is sure to be at odds with his surroundings at every step he takes. He is like a fish on the beach or a bird with a broken wing. He will find himself hampered and hobbled; and he will be baffled, irritated, and rebellious. He will get to hate the life and everything and everyone in it. He is, by some psychological twist, wholly unaware that it is all his own fault, that he made an initial and essential mistake when he chose the life as he would choose a club, or a literary or scientific society, or a group of university dons. Again, the ex-Jesuit, who turns upon his former associates, may have started his life in the Society with the right intention and gradually drifted away from it until his original purpose was completely lost. The supernatural point of view is a grace of God which requires the cooperation of a prayerful vigilance to preserve it against the encroachments of a crowding worldliness. The result is the same in both cases.

Plain living and high thinking used to be the boast of literary Concord. It is a brave philosophy. Plain living is not so attractive if the high thinking is absent. And nowhere is high thinking more indispensable as an adjunct of plain living than in the religious life. When the high thinking ceases in the Society of Jesus or any other similar society, the religious life becomes a shoddy and tawdry mode of existence which it is easy to hold up to scorn and execration.

It is hard to find any honorable ground for these so-called exposures. The writer of them was not obliged to enter the Society; and, after he had entered, he was not compelled to remain. From the very beginning, he was made acquainted with the nature and aims of the life he had freely embraced.

If, by any chance, he was inveigled into it by misunderstanding and false representations, he had ample time to reconsider his step. To go through two years of novitiate and eight or nine years of studies, and, perhaps, a longer time in various occupations, and then to shake the dust of a religious house off his feet, and, instead of finding any cause for blame in himself where the blame lies, to seek a public outlet for his injured feelings and proceed to write and publish a book which will appeal to the enemies of religion more than to its friends, all this must seem a petty performance in the eyes of a thoughtful reader.

I shall attempt here to describe how it happens that such a man can give what may seem to him to be a truthful picture which as a matter of fact is utterly false. It is false because it represents as a sort of hell on earth a life which thousands of men in the past and present have found to be a very vestibule of heaven, a peaceful haven, a place for dear associations, pure memories, gentle companionship, high inspiration, and rich opportunities for employing one's little talent in the noblest of causes.

The first inclination of anyone in the religious life, who never had the supernatural point of view, or who is losing it, is to evade as far as possible everything that bears down unpleasantly upon human nature. He will become secretive, politic, deceitful, as the occasion rises, to attain his ends. He is told that the life of perfection, to which he has committed himself, imposes on him the obligation of patiently learning to regard his superior as bearing the person of Christ and to accept his wishes as expressive of God's will. But the naturalist in religion sneers at such pietistic simplicity, despises those who practise it, and regards all superiors as his natural enemies. If he cannot circumvent them, he will be in a constant feud with them. There will be reprimands and scenes. A superior has a grave obligation in conscience to enforce rules, to see that they are not treated flippantly, and deliberately and habitually ignored. The rules are the substantial props of the Society: if their neglect ever became a commonplace practice, the whole superstructure would tumble in ruins about the ears not only of the offending parties but also of those who in good faith have sought a refuge under them and who strive to hold them in respect.

Moreover, the rules do for the religious life what the laws of social life do for the world. Their observance makes life together not only endurable but pleasant. No one can help seeing what a cat's fight social life would be in terms of an unbridled individualism. The integrity, the happiness, the very existence of religious life depend on the vigilance and firmness of superiors, and a cheerful cooperation with them. If for no other reason, superiors owe it to their fellow religious to discourage laxity, especially if it is less a matter of human weakness than a contempt of rules, arising from a contempt of the whole supernatural philosophy of the religious life.

Superiors in the Society practise great patience and indulgence. But it must be obvious that there will be situations in which indulgence beyond certain limits would increase the evil. And so the man who goes in for naturalism will arrive at a stage where he will not be trusted, and will be watched to prevent him from bringing trouble and disgrace upon his associates. He will feel harassed, hounded, and persecuted; and, after he leaves the Society, he will enlarge in his book on the subject of espionage as a conspicuously active element in the Society, tending to develop a demoralizing atmosphere of talebearing, secret spite, and hypocrisy.

Espionage is a telling point. It is an odious word and suggests odious things to all lovers of honor and free institutions. And the ex-Jesuit can here put the Jesuits themselves in the witness box on the side of the accuser. One of their rules explicitly states that everyone must be content to have his faults made known by others to superiors. On its face this rule seems to afford grounds for everything the accuser has to say about espionage in the Society. Does it? Let us see.

In the first place, the accuser was informed of this rule when he entered the Society and, by remaining in the Society, accepted it and agreed to abide by it. I do not see anything dishonorable or unmanly in a group of persons agreeing among themselves to tell one another directly or indirectly of their faults with a view of improving their lives severally and collectively. Every large business concern encourages and keeps reports of its personnel without asking their leave, and no one thinks it dishonorable. It would seem to be a necessary provision in any large body of men whose security and reputation depended more or less on the integrity of every man in it. As for the Society, the common run of Jesuits have little or no occasion to advert to such a thing as espionage. During my fifty years as a Jesuit, I have never been asked to spy on anyone. I do not say it boastfully; I am merely stating a fact. Another fact that has come under my notice is that Jesuit superiors know how to deal with the natural-born talebearer; he gets little encouragement. The nearest thing to espionage in my experience are the *informationes* which are sent to Rome when the General is considering some Jesuit for an important superiorship. They are questionnaires which are sent in confidence to a few, who happen to have lived in the same community with the man under consideration, in which they are asked to give an opinion on his fitness for a highly responsible post.

It is quite probable that there has been too little, rather than too much, espionage in the Society. I say this with reference not only to the interests and good name of the Society, but also to the best interests and happiness of the embittered ex-Jesuit. If he had been more carefully watched and corrected at the beginning of his career, he might not have become faithless to his high vocation. Superiors in the Society like to suppose that every man has a sense of his own responsibility which will make him cultivate and preserve the supernatural point of view by fidelity to his rules and by habits of prayer. After all, it is the subject's own business more than someone else's. If he is recalcitrant and withdraws from the Society, the most unjust thing he can do is to blame the Society and its superiors. The ex-Jesuit, who denounces surveillance, took his first false step in evading it: he found it a very easy thing to do.

As a rule, ex-Jesuits remain friendly with the Society. Some of them ceased to be Jesuits through no fault of theirs. But, even in cases when they were dismissed from the Society, they have been known to have harbored no ill feeling. I shall give striking instances in the two following chapters.

CHAPTER 20

GRESSET, EX-JESUIT AND POET

JEAN BAPTISTE LOUIS GRESSET is a notable figure in the history of French literature. His *Le Méchant* is a classic comedy, and he ranks with France's best writers of light and humorous poetry. He was born at Amiens in 1709, and, after his boyhood education in a Jesuit school, entered the Society at the age of sixteen. He made his philosophical studies in the famous Collège Louis le Grand, and was then sent to teach in the Jesuit college in Rouen.

In 1734, while he was still in Rouen, his *Vert-Vert* — more accurately, *Ver-Vert,* that is, "Gray-Green" — appeared and threw France, and indeed all Europe, into gales of laughter. Written in witty decasyllabics, it told the story of a parrot in a Visitation convent. The apt bird had learned from the nuns many pious phrases, and its reputation for decorum grew until another convent begged to be allowed to have him for a brief visit. On the way down the canal, the parrot picked up the profanity of the bargemen with results that may be imagined on his arrival at his destination. He was shipped back in a hurry to his home and subjected to a course of penance until he learned better. And then he died from overfeeding.

The poem was composed in high spirits, and the fun in it is irresistible. It suited the mood of a world that always takes religion lightly and regards convent life as too quaint for words. A sister of the powerful de Chauvelin, Keeper of the Seals, was a Visitation nun, and she complained to her brother, not unreasonably, about this Jesuit publication. In the mean-time, Gresset had come to Paris from Rouen to make his theological studies in the Collège Louis le Grand. It is difficult to believe that Gresset, still a young scholastic, had published the poem with the usual official approval. But the worst critics of "Jesuit fanaticism" must confess that all through his troubles Gresset was treated with lenient forbearance by his superiors.

When de Chauvelin lodged his protest with the Provincial, Gresset was taken from his course of theology in Paris and bundled off to La Flèche, another famous Jesuit college, the alma mater of Descartes and David Hume, where he was given the honorable post of Professor of Rhetoric. Being remote from the capital and in the country, it was probably considered a safer sort of domicile for that dangerous thing called genius. Anyhow, it was a mild punishment. At least, de Chauvelin might forget about him. In most of the notices of Gresset, which have appeared in English, the impression is conveyed that the Jesuits expelled Gresset from the Order for having written a masterpiece of gay humor. It is true, some of the fathers thought he ought to be expelled; but, in view of his youth and his repentant mood, superiors were content with exile to La Flèche.

But the mercurial temperament of the artist could not be repressed. In the following year, Gresset got himself into a worse tangle. His *La Chartreuse* appeared in print without authorization. Gresset may have been in good faith when he pleaded innocence of any conscious violation of his rule in the publication of his poems. But, after one disastrous precedent, it is not easy to understand how he could have counted on the discretion of admiring friends among whom his manuscripts were freely circulated. This time the matter was more serious: he offended the Paris *parlement,* a far more powerful and dangerous body than a convent of nuns.

The *parlement* of Paris was composed of nobles, ecclesiastics, and rich commoners, and exercised judicial and administrative powers which made them a strong element in the government of France. In fact, it was the highest tribunal of justice in the land. It could, on occasion, force the hand of the King and his ministers of state. It was the inveterate enemy of the Jesuits, whose teaching and influence were opposed to its extreme nationalism in all matters pertaining to the government of the Church in France. The *parlement* was an alert foe, not always scrupulous in its methods of attack, and one the Jesuits were careful not to arouse except on some serious challenge of its loyalty to the Church.

It was this body of men that was the target of a satirical passage in *La Chartreuse*. When a published copy of the poem came under the notice of the Jesuits, it created serious misgivings. The Provincial wrote a hasty letter to Cardinal de Fleury, the first minister of state:

Monseigneur: I have the honor of writing to Your Eminence on a matter which is of concern to us. We have a young man named Gresset who possesses a genuine talent in French poetry. He has before this been guilty of indiscretion in allowing to get into print a poem containing some very reprehensible passages. When his superiors were apprised of this, they withdrew him from Paris where he was studying theology and sent him to La Flèche. Some were even of the opinion that he ought to be dismissed from the Society; but others, touched by his repentance and his promise to make no more French verses except at the request of his superiors, thought that a less severe penalty should be imposed. But today we learn that, besides the first piece which came to our attention, he has done a second which contains verses of a kind to stir the indignation of the *parlement,* and not without reason. This piece has fallen into the hands of a publisher who has had it printed; but M. Hérault (the lieutenant-general of police) by his vigilance and out of his friendship for us, has suppressed its circulation. Still, it is to be feared that eagerness for profits will eventually provide a way for its sale and distribution. Then, not to be exposed to all the mischievous consequences which the poem can draw down upon us from the side of the *parlement,* we should be obliged to give his dismissal to the author. If Your Eminence wishes to confer with M. Hérault, you will see better than we what we ought to do.

The Cardinal sent this letter to M. Hérault, with the notation that the young man had undoubtedly a wonderful gift for poetry, but "he allows himself too much freedom and will certainly bring the Jesuits into trouble unless they get rid of him. The simple thing to do, and the surest, is to dismiss him." M. Hérault forwarded the Cardinal's advice to the Jesuits and Gresset had to go.

I think it will be clear from all this that the Paris *parlement* had more to do with Gresset's expulsion than any harsh attitude of the Society toward literary genius. Yet I doubt whether any account of Gresset's career that has appeared in English has ever mentioned this salient fact. The writer of the article on Gresset in the eleventh edition of the *Encyclopaedia Britannica* says of Gresset's dismissal from the Order: "Men of robust mind would have been glad to get rid of such a yoke. Gresset, who had never been glad to stand alone, went forth weeping."

The gibe is directed undoubtedly to the famous poem written by Gresset after his dismissal, and entitled *Adieux aux Jésuites.* The following is a literal translation of a part of it:

Yes, in the sundering of my bonds I am filled with regret; I meet freedom coldly.

I look back mournfully at the noble companionship I have quitted; I am sorrow-stricken for the holy intercourse no longer mine.

If I am no more to be found by their firesides, my heart continues to dwell among them.

For you must not take them as envious hand and jaundiced eye portray them.

If you know them only as the clouds of calumny distort them, you know them not at all.

Read and note in their daily life how genuinely straightfor-word they are.

It gives me unbounded satisfaction to be able to speak out about them.

No self-interest, no fear, no hope prompts me; for my lot is no longer cast with theirs; it is an impartial hand that traces the picture.

Yes, I have seen men — I must here avow it — too often op-posed, too often misunderstood.

I have seen high-minded men, pure hearts, devoted to their country, their king, and their God; indifferent to their own ills, prodigal of their days, tender-hearted and perfect friends, and often the quiet benefactors of their most outrageous ene-mies; in a word, men too highly esteemed not to be as ferociously hated.

Let others who, even as I, go out from among them, vent their senseless spleen in mischievous attacks designed to make them hated.

As for me, cleaving to the truth and faithful to my own soul, I speak this parting word of fond farewell.

After his departure from the Society, Gresset naturally turned to literature for a career, and specifically to the theater. His serious plays were not marked successes; but his comedy, *Le Méchant,* met with enthusiastic applause and still holds the stage, Brunetière declaring it to be the best comedy of its kind in that century. Gresset was elected to the French Academy in 1748, not a small honor for a man still in the thirties. Frederick II invited him to join the coterie of French men of letters at the Prussian court, but Gresset had no relish for the Voltairean color of his compatriots there and declined. In 1759 he retired to his native city of Amiens and spent the remain-ing eighteen years of his life in strict seclusion, living a peni-tential life for having abandoned his early spiritual ideals.

Beneath the surface gaiety of Gresset, there must have been a solid core of seriousness and solid piety. It may be true that he had not "the minimum of gravity required of a Jesuit," but the obvious reluctance of his superiors to dismiss him, and his own reluctance to be dismissed, indicate the presence in him of something deeper than thoughtless frivolity. His voluntary withdrawal from Paris and the sunshine of popular favor, while still in his prime, to spend his last years in prayerful retirement is another sign that his impish wit had not wholly got the better of a deeply devout spirit.

CHAPTER 21

FATHER PROUT

IN HIS career and in the playful turn of his genius, Francis Sylvester Mahony, better known as "Father Prout," reminds one of Gresset, of whose *Vert-Vert* he has given us a lively metrical translation. Little more of Mahony is remembered today than that he is the author of that pleasant classic, *The Bells of Shandon.* Yet he was a distinguished figure in the literary London of the first half of the nineteenth century, and his *Reliques of Father Prout* is a minor classic that assures him of at least a paler sort of immortality. It is a veritable curiosity shop of wit, humor, metrical surprises, satire, keen observation and gleanings of vast literary erudition of a cosmopolitan kind. In a low state of classical culture its jovial freedom with the authors of antiquity would, it is to be feared, create more bewilderment than entertainment. Charles Lamb, I think, would have reveled in its pages; but Charles died the very year the *Reliques* began to appear in *Fraser's Magazine.*

For detailed information about Mahony the reader is referred to the fairly extensive sketch by Sir Sidney Lee in the *Dictionary of National Biography.* Lee is somewhat vague, and almost certainly inaccurate, in his account of Mahony's early life; once he has got Mahony to London, he is probably more trustworthy.

Francis Sylvester Mahony was born in Cork in 1804. His father was a prosperous manufacturer and sent the boy to be educated by the Jesuits, first in Clongowes Wood, and later in their College of St. Acheul at Amiens. There Francis decided to become a Jesuit and he entered the Paris novitiate and after-

wards went for his studies to Rome. He became noted for his
ease and mastery in writing Latin verse and prose and in
speaking Latin. He must have attracted some attention outside
the Order by his brilliant attainments. Lee quotes from a book,
Les Jésuits Modernes, published in Paris, 1826, and written by
Abbé Martial Marcet de la Roché-Arnaud, an enemy of the
Jesuits, in which the author tells of having met the young
Jesuit in Rome and goes on to say that "he had all the fanaticism, the dissimulation, the intrigue, and the chicanery" usually met with in Jesuits.

In 1830 Mahony was appointed Prefect and Master of
Rhetoric in Clongowes Wood; but a cross-country excursion
with some of his pupils to Maynooth, from which they returned at midnight in convivial spirits, terminated his brief
period of teaching. He went first to the Jesuit house at Freiburg
and then to Florence where he received his formal dismissal
from the Society. It was a disgrace keenly felt. That he never
after harbored resentment against the Order, and seized opportunities, as in his essay on *Literature and the Jesuits,* to praise
it, speaks equally well for him and the Jesuits. It is highly
probable that it was more than the indiscretion of a single
misadventure which brought about his expulsion. His temper
and disposition did not fit easily into the pattern of the religious life. He was singularly independent in his views and at
the same time reckless of when and how he expressed them.
Thus, while in Ireland, he gloried in shocking the popular
idolatry of Daniel O'Connell, whom he loathed — probably,
for purely literary reasons.

Against the advice of his friends, he went to Rome to study
for the secular clergy and was ordained in 1832. It was a mistake which he lived to regret. He returned as a priest to his
native town and did heroic service as chaplain of a hospital
during a severe and prolonged plague of cholera. Owing to a
quarrel with his bishop over the construction of a church, he
left Cork and went to London where he shortly afterwards

gave up the exercise of his priesthood and merged himself in the bohemian life of literary circles.

In April, 1834, he began his connection with *Fraser's Magazine*, which was beginning to win its position as the foremost English monthly of the day; Carlyle's *Sartor Resartus* had just appeared in preceding numbers. Sir Sidney Lee says of Mahony's contributions: "The brilliance of the papers helped to establish *Fraser's Magazine* on a firm basis, and secured for the author a wide reputation." Mahony's problem at the start of his career was one of tact. He was writing for the British public of the thirties, a public still steeped in the Protestant tradition, disdainfully hostile even in its upper strata to the stream of Catholic culture which had civilized Europe. From that stream Mahony had drawn most of his literary resources. How could he employ them before a suspicious public jealously on its guard against whatever might conceivably be regarded as papistical propaganda?

His solution of the problem was as ingenious as it was happy, one that gave play to the attainments of the priest without betraying him. He created the character of Father Prout, an old Irish parish priest of Watergrasshill, County Cork, a Catholic counterpart of the Vicar of Wakefield. A genial recluse abounding in the most varied learning, a kindly mixture of simplicity and shrewdness, who watched the world from afar with a sharp critical eye and wrote his impressions edged with satire, with just a touch of the garrulous pedantry to be expected in the circumstances, and a facile versifier in half a dozen languages, he was interesting in himself and in the reminiscences of interesting persons whom he had met abroad before his retirement to an obscure parish. He is introduced to us in person by Mahony, signing himself "Oliver Yorke," in the first of the papers, which ends with a notice of the old priest's death and funeral and some Latin memorial pentameters, accompanied by a translation in English iambics. In this introductory paper the way is prepared for the other papers which purport to be gems rescued from the chest to which Father Prout had been wont to consign his literary productions.

The hilarious tone which "Oliver Yorke" employed to keep his English audience in good humor may be gathered from the account of how the chest was conveyed to London:

> We owe it to the public to account for the delay experienced in the transmission of the "chest" from Watergrasshill to our hands. The fact is, that at a meeting of the parishioners held on the subject (Mat Horrogan, of Blarney, in the chair) it was *resolved*, "That Terry Callaghan, being a tall and trustworthy man, able to do credit to the village in London, and carry eleven stone weight (the precise tariff of the trunk), should be sent at the public expense, *via* Bristol, with the coffer strapped to his shoulders, and plenty of the wherewithal to procure 'refreshment' on the western road, until he should deliver the same at Mr. Fraser's, Regent Street, with the compliments of the parish." Terry, wisely considering, like the Commissioners of the Decan prize-money, that the occupation was too good a thing not to make it last as long as possible, kept refreshing himself, at the cost of the parochial committee, on the great western road, and only arrived last week in Regent Street. . . . Here, then, we are enabled, no longer deferring the promised boon, to lay before the public the first of the "Prout Papers"; breaking, to use a seaman's phrase, and producing at hazard a specimen of what is contained in the coffer brought hither on the shoulders of tall and trustworthy Terry Callaghan.
>
> *Pandere res alta Terra et Caligine mersas.*

The reader will note how tall Terry Callaghan is embedded, like a bee in amber, in the limpid Virgilian line.

But, mixed with the irresponsible nonsense, of a kind only a cultivated mind could perpetrate, there was much wise reflection, penetrating criticism, literary and religious information, in these papers. One of Mahony's pet aversions was Tom Moore whose candied style he never tired of ridiculing. In his paper on *The Rogueries of Tom Moore,* he impudently accuses

Moore of the grossest plagiarisms from Greek, Latin, and French poets, giving the poems in the original tongues and printing them with Moore's in deadly parallels. He charges Moore with even having stolen from Father Prout himself. Father Prout is made to say how he once showed a juvenile performance to Tom, beginning

> *Lesbia semper hinc et inde*
> *Oculorum tela movit;*
> *Captat omnes, sed deinde*
> *Quis ametur nemo novit.*

What was his astonishment to find Tom coming out with

> Lesbia hath a beaming eye,
>   But no one knows for whom it beameth;
> Right and left the arrows fly,
>   But what they aim at, no one dreameth.

The hoax was not altogether ineffective, and it is said that Moore was seriously annoyed, a result that would not disturb Mahony.

In his paper on *Literature and the Jesuits,* he manages to put in a good word for his former associates, reminding his public that it is a foolish thing to speak about people and things about which they know little or nothing. The first sentence of this paper is interesting in view of recent happenings: "The massacre this month by a brutal populace in Madrid of four-teen Jesuits, in the hall of their college of St. Isodoro, has drawn somewhat of notice, if not of sympathy, to this singular order of literati." The *Reliques* came to an end in *Fraser's* during 1836, and were published in two volumes, with many illustrations by the famous Maclise, a fellow townsman of Mahony. The frontispiece, regularly appearing in subsequent single-volume editions, is the well-known cartoon of Maclise, picturing a dinner table surrounded by the Fraserians at one of their periodical festivals. Here we have remarkable likenesses of Thackeray, Southey, S. T. Coleridge, Lockhart, Carlyle, and lesser lights of the day. Mahony, wearing spectacles, looks kindly and benignant, although Sir Sidney Lee declares that he had personally "less amiability than is proverbial with Irish humorists."

It is to be feared that Mahony was never to be very happy in spite of his assured position among London men of letters. He became a friend and associate of Dickens, and was welcome at Lady Blessington's and the literary clubs, but it is recorded that he was not happy. He was at different times Roman correspondent for Dickens's *Daily News;* Paris correspondent to the *Globe* for many years up to his death; a prominent contributor to the *Cornhill Magazine* and the *Athenaeum,* and the author of another book. He had toured eastern Europe and Asia Minor for three years in the late thirties; and, after changing his domicile often, finally settled down in Paris in 1848, where he lived alone without a servant in obscure lodgings till his death, May 18, 1866. His sister, Mrs. Woodlock — two of her grandsons are Jesuits — attended him in his last illness, and he was buried in the vaults of Shandon Church in Cork. Three years before, he had petitioned Rome for laicization; his petition was granted, and, because of failing eyesight and advancing age, he was dispensed from daily office in the breviary, to say the rosary and penitential psalms instead.

In *Literature and the Jesuits* he reprehends the historian Robertson for saying that St. Ignatius was a mere fanatic who had no idea he was founding a great Order.

> Never did the historian adopt a more egregious blunder. Had he had the leisure or patience to con over the original code, called Institutum Soc. Jesu, he would have found in every paragraph of that profound and crafty [a Fraser interpolation? the word does not match this cloth.] volume the germs of wondrous future development. . . . Yes, the mind of Loyola lies embalmed in the leaves of that mystic tome; and the ark of cedar-wood, borne by the children of Israel

along the sands of the desert, was not more essential to their happy progress unto the land of promise than that grand depository of the founder's wisdom was to the march of intellect among the Jesuits.

In the same paper he gives us some Latin alcaics in praise of St. Ignatius, with a spirited English metrical version, the last stanza of which, describing the result of Loyola's vigil at Montserrat, runs as follows:

> India repaired half Europe's loss;
> O'er a new hemisphere the Cross
>   Shone in the azure sky;
> And, from the isles of far Japan
> To the broad Andes, won o'er man
>   A bloodless victory.

It would seem that Mahony never could forget his old associations nor reconcile himself wholly to their loss. We can indulge the hope that St. Ignatius met him at the last with a touch of paternal recognition.

CHAPTER 22

THE JESUIT AND OTHER SOCIETIES
IN THE CHURCH

THE Jesuit, it may be stated at once, thinks that his own
Order is the best in the world — for him. It was through
it that the vocation to the religious life came to him. If there
had been no Society of Jesus, he might in all probability never
have attempted to consecrate himself entirely to God's service.
It presented to his youthful mind an ideal that attracted his
particular temper and character. It took him and molded him
with patient wisdom into something like the man he aspired
to be. And, after many years, he looks back over a past which
it has filled with innocence and white memories, with victories
over his own difficult nature, with quiet and peaceful hours
after desolating conflicts, with chances and opportunities of
doing a good stroke now and then, in his own feeble way,
for Christ and His Church in a world that does not know
where truth and the soul's best interests lie. The beauty and
splendor of Christ and His Church have been revealed to him
by his gracious mother, the Society. May she keep him and
conduct him all the way to the feet of Him whose name she
bears. And may oblivion descend swiftly upon him and blot
him out from the land of the living if he ever forget her
claims upon his grateful devotion.

That is the way a Jesuit regards the Society of Jesus.

And it is not only my ardent hope, but also my confident
belief, that every member of other Religious Orders and Congregations, and every member of the secular clergy, regards
his own special following of Christ in the same way.

No reasonable person will see an implicit criticism of other religious bodies in the profound love a Jesuit has for the Society. A man's love for his mother carries no slighting undertone of disrespect for the mothers of other men; it does not lead him to think scornfully of them, or to suppress sentiments of the greatest admiration for their virtues and accomplishments. With this primary fact understood, is there any foundation for the alleged jealousy of Jesuits for all those doing the work of God outside their own Order? Do they go about among people making disparaging remarks about Benedictines, Dominicans, Franciscans, Servites, Passionists, diocesan clergy? Do they belittle all religious work except their own? Do they carry themselves with a superior air, and, when the achievements of others are introduced, "damn with faint praise, assent with civil sneer"? Do they conform to what Chesterton calls "the picture of the evil of the literary temperament"? Does the Jesuit, like Addison,

> Bear, like the Turk, no brother near the throne,
> View him with scornful, yet with jealous eyes,
> And hate for arts that caused himself to rise?

Do Jesuits go into conspiratorial huddles to find and execute measures for undermining the good influence of rival institutions? One could go on for pages drawing up the list of similar charges made against Jesuits. Is there any serious ground for these charges?

If these charges are made against the Society as a whole, they can be dismissed as the idle vaporings of fanatical enemies. When St. Ignatius wished his Society to call itself the "least Society," he was not indulging in sanctimonious humility. He hated, in his Society, anything like a bumptious self-complacence, either corporately or individually. Readers of his life will not need to be told how genuine and sincere were his admiration and reverence for other Orders. He considered that no one could be a good Catholic if he did not "praise

greatly religious Orders and a life of virginity and continency."
It is only fair that the Society should, like every other body,
be judged by principles not by instances. The Institute of the
Society, its Constitutions and rules, its ordinations of Generals
and its literature, are open books at the disposal of anyone who
seeks to find in them any official encouragement of a policy of
belittlement or opposition toward other religious organizations.

The Jesuits of St. Ignatius' time found it easy to take his
broad and enlightened view of their position in the Church.
They formed a new and infant Order, with a scheme of life
notably different from that of the older Orders and specially
designed to meet and overcome new dangers to the Catholic
Church. But we see no evidence that they regarded the older
Orders as superannuated institutions. There was work for all.
They knew that the Catholic Church, to use Newman's words,
"did not lose Benedict by finding Dominic; and she still has
both Benedict and Dominic at home, though she has become
the mother of Ignatius."

I do not deny that some Jesuit or other can be cited in support of these charges. If there be such a Jesuit, I have no
hesitation in saying he is not a representative Jesuit. Instead
of proving that the Society has an unpleasantly emulative spirit,
it seems to me he proves that the Society is not so successful
in eradicating the human in a man as its enemies proclaim.
The various religious societies in the Church are much like
the regiments in an army: if an irresponsible gascon thinks
that the honor of his own regiment requires him to abuse all
others, no one takes him seriously. It has even been known
that an Oxford man can be politely disagreeable whenever
Cambridge is mentioned: and conversely. If the members of
religious societies succumb to this petty weakness, it argues an
absence of the historic sense as much as of charity and humility.

Father John Roothaan was the third General of the Society
after its restoration in 1814. He was elected General in 1829.
He was a man who united unusual intellectual accomplish-

ments with rare executive capacity and deep spirituality. He had become a Jesuit while the Society, or what had been left of it, was confined to Russia; and, on becoming General, arduously employed all his great talents and spiritual resources to recover for the new Society the spirit of the old in all its plenitude. For this purpose, he produced a valuable work on the Exercises of St. Ignatius, and issued a notable series of letters to the whole Society. In one of these letters, dated from Rome, July 7, 1830, and entitled, "Letter to the Fathers and Brothers of the Society of Jesus on the Love of Our Society and Institute" he takes cognizance of the reproach which malevolent critics so often leveled at the old Society. This letter is read annually in the refectory of every Jesuit community; it cannot exactly be called a dead letter.

"Here comes for consideration another evil which I would fain keep far from all of us, which by itself would shut off from the Society the abundance of God's gifts if, God forbid, it should find a home in the hearts of Ours. It has not escaped you, Reverend Fathers and dear Brothers in Christ, how often our people have been accused of pride and vainglory, and how often it has been harped on, that the men of the Society, most humble though they have been individually, have nevertheless been most proud with regard to the Society at large and have been prone to look down upon those not of the Society, to belittle their merits, to envy their success, to care nothing for what has been done by others than Ours and, in a word, to act as if they imagined that all learning, all virtue, all real service for God and the neighbor were found in the Society alone.

"I am not, indeed, ignorant that these charges are utterly unfounded with regard to our men commonly, and have been trumped up with a view to bring hatred upon the Society; yet, were only one among us of this mind, I would consider it cause for the deepest grief and would apprehend great harm for the whole Society through the fault of one of its members.

Is it possible that anyone can bring himself to think that conduct, which would be for the individual a disgrace and a fault before God, will be justified, will be virtue and loyalty, simply because it glorifies not the individual but the Society?
. . . I fear much that those who speak most of the glory of the Society, as they call it, and make the glory of the Society their sole theme, are much like those persons who boast of the high rank of their families but are themselves unworthy scions and poor samples of the glory of their ancestors. Thus one will sometimes see men lauding to the skies the association they belong to, imagining they are more than rich enough in the honors their predecessors have won, while they never dream of making a contribution of their own; fancying, indeed, that those very honors entitle them to lead a life of ease and repose. . . .

"Is not the greater glory of God the scope, the goal of our whole life, of all our studies, of all our labors? And, if we are sincere in our purpose, should not every successful work for the glory of God, whosoever does it, be matter of congratulation for us? God grant the day when all religious of whatever Order and all men of apostolic life will strive together as one man for the good of the Church with all the strength they are capable of and with the most complete success. Truly the times are such and the needs of Christian States so great that the laborers in God's vineyard could be multiplied and room and opportunity still be left for doing the work of God and His Church. . . .

"However, Reverend Fathers and dear Brothers in Christ, I cannot bring myself to believe that any one of you would display his love of the Society by conduct which is in open conflict with the spirit of the Society. Yet, I wished to touch on these points which are often urged against us in these carping times, that each of us may not by word or act incur the suspicion of pride or jealousy, that Ours in all lands may love and honor those who have taken up and promote the cause of God, that they may cherish with proper reverence and sincere affection the members of every other religious family, and, especially, of such Orders as, for centuries before the Society, made glorious the Church of God by their learning and achievements and have never ceased to deserve well of the Church; in a word, I have said what I have, that Ours may keep in mind that humility and charity are the chief glories of our Society and that they should not bear such a love of the Society as is opposed to her teaching, such as would harm rather than help her, such as would impede rather than hasten her growth, such as would utterly destroy her."

This letter ought to have some effect on the gascons of the regiment if they turn up somewhere.

Monsignor Hanly in his interesting "Life of Pignatelli" cites an instance of the relations between Jesuits and one of the older Orders. Giuseppi Pignatelli was beatified in 1933. He was a member of the Society at the time of its suppression, and spent long laborious years trying to keep the shattered fragments of the Society together till such time as might allow them to be welded again into their former integrity. The Duke of Parma invited Father Pignatelli and some of his former associates to start a novitiate at Colorno in 1799. The Duke did this, it is said, with the verbal permission of the Pope. Shortly after its foundation, Napoleon stepped in to crush the young enterprise. Father Pignatelli was the novice-master during its brief existence, and one of the novices under him, probably the one who afterwards became the famous Cardinal Mai, left some reminiscences which make pleasant reading. Here is a passage from them:

"Father Pignatelli had a particular liking for the venerable Order of Dominicans and gave proof of this predilection. Saint Dominic's picture occupied a prominent place above his prie-dieu. And the Dominicans of Colorno returned his fellow feeling. The relations between their house and ours could not have been more cordial. On the respective feasts of the founders, a Jesuit always preached on Saint Dominic in their church, and a Dominican on Saint Ignatius in ours. The novices of the two houses frequently entertained one another and took long walks together. The good prince, Duke Ferdinand, was a common father to us. He was happiest when he could bring us together on his spacious grounds and serve us with refreshments. One great event, to which we were always invited, was Founder's Day at the Dominican house in honor of Duke Ferdinand. It was then a real pleasure to watch the keen delight with which our novice-master took his place as server at the table of the Dominican novices."

There have been controversies between Jesuits and other Orders — there still are — and sometimes they have been acrimonious. I need not recount them for the simple reason that they are the only side of the relations of Jesuits with other Orders that popular historians love to dwell upon. Everyone knows about them. It is needless to say that in these controversies both parties were moved by conscientious allegiance to truth and the Church. If there were faults, they were faults of excessive zeal in a good cause. Less is known by the public at large of the many pleasant passages between the Orders that are of almost daily occurrence. I have cited one such passage, and I could cite many more. In the spiritual diary of the late Pierre Bouscaren, one of the entries runs as follows: "Monday, Sept. 8, 1911. Feast of the Stigmata of St. Francis Assisi. I pray for the Franciscans today, and I ask St. Francis to pray for the Jesuits, that they too and his children may be saints — great saints."

As for the Jesuits and the secular clergy, their normal relations are most amicable. If there be anywhere a Jesuit who looks down upon secular priests, I would say that, from the mere standpoint of intelligence, he is a poor specimen of his Order. The present reigning Pontiff was a secular priest. So were his great and holy predecessors, Pius XI, Benedict XV, Pius X, Leo XIII, and Pius IX, to go back no farther. If I am not mistaken, most of the names prominent in modern English Catholic literature, beginning with John Lingard, are those of secular priests. A secular priest may, for the most part, have to create as best he can in a busy life, his own facilities for advancing in religious perfection, and this interior life of holiness can be taken for granted in the case of every priest whose sacerdotal character is the most distinctive thing about him. It is only to be expected that the ranks of those whose mode of life produced a St. Francis of Sales and a Curé d'Ars will have numerous instances of hidden sanctity.

There have been controversies between Jesuits and the secular clergy, as there have been between Jesuits and other Orders. Most of them arise from what may be called overlapping jurisdictions more or less inherent in the constitution of the Church. But in these controversies zeal for the Church is the prevailing motive rather than any hostile animus. When trouble crops up, I have a suspicion that it is started and kept alive by the friends of both parties. The houses of Capulet and Montagu might have been more cordial to each other were it not for the misguided zeal of their followers.

CHAPTER 23

EMINENCE IN THE SOCIETY

THE energy and activity of the Society in fields of secular endeavor — in literature and the sciences — may seem difficult to reconcile with the comparatively small value it attaches to fame and reputation in those pursuits. All its exhortations are directed to the spiritual progress of its members. Its rules and constitutions all but ignore any other kind of progress; whenever intellectual studies are mentioned, they are referred to almost grudgingly as minor incidents, important in their way as useful instruments in spiritual work, but not without suspicion of being dampers of ardor and sappers of the spirit. The only honors the Society has to bestow — and they are posthumous — are those won by sanctity of life. If eminence in the arts and sciences be present as well as eminence in holiness, so much the better, perhaps; because in that case the Jesuit brought the gold, frankincense, and myrrh of intellectual accomplishments to the adoration of the Creator, a service to which rich gifts are too seldom devoted. But, whether it be an angel, a king, or a shepherd, adoration and service are the main things; all else is secondary and even negligible.

The Society is always ready to welcome the owner of talents and skill as long as they contribute to something more than a sense of his own importance. Not every man can be an Aquinas, a Dante, or a Newton; but he can become, or aspire to become, a saint. If he aspire to be less, be he never so distinguished, the Society will not hang his picture in its hall of fame.

Not that the Society encourages mediocrity or suffers fools

gladly. It expects its members in every grade to show the presence of a brain and to cultivate it according to the measure of their opportunity; and, when the Society gives the opportunity, it is not pleased if they neglect it. But, while intellectual promise is among the favorable conditions for admission, in the case of candidates for the priesthood, it is regarded as less precious than qualities of character.

In the second of the rules for these candidates, called scholastics, one can observe that character is aimed at as well as intellectual proficiency. While the young men are cautioned not to allow absorption in study to cool their love of solid virtue and the religious life, they are at the same time to bear in mind that, keeping their spiritual integrity intact, they can do nothing more pleasing to God than to be diligent with their books. The rule declares that divine pleasure is not less if application and perseverance are exercised on studies which the student is convinced he will never find useful in his future work.

St. John Berchmans, who died while he was a scholastic, was canonized because he was a living embodiment of the rules of the Society. It is interesting to see how he illustrated this second rule in practice. In Father Albert S. Foley's life of the saint, we can read the testimony of Father Piccolomini, Berchman's teacher in philosophy. "Berchmans, besides excellent talents which were capable of taking in a number of different subjects at the same time, possessed an ardor and industry such as no one, in my opinion, ever surpassed and few are able to equal. He was eager to become proficient in all subjects even if they would be of no use to him. . . . And he spared no time or effort to master various languages and sciences and everything that goes to make a learned and erudite man."

The question of just how far this attitude has operated to bring out or suppress genius and talent in the Society is a question that has received much attention from friends and enemies. It would seem on the face of it that men, who sub-ordinate excellence in the arts and sciences to something they think far more important, would not go so far as men who make such excellence a lifework that absorbs ambition and energies with the possessiveness of a passionate devotion. Per-haps some light can be thrown upon the matter by passages from the writings of two keen observers whose views have the large perspective of an authentic historical survey. The first of these passages is from Newman's essay on the "Mission of St. Benedict," in which he describes the characteristics of three great teaching Orders in the history of the Church. "Coming now," he says, "to the historical proof of the con-trast I have been instituting, I am sanguine in thinking that one branch of it is already allowed by the consent of the world, and is undeniable. By common consent, the palm of religious Prudence, in the Aristotelic sense of that comprehen-sive word, belongs to the School of Religion of which St. Ignatius is the Founder. That great Society is the classical seat and fountain (that is, in religious thought and the conduct of life, for of ecclesiastical politics I speak not), the school and pattern of discretion, practical sense, and wise government. Sublimer conceptions or more profound speculations may have been created or elaborated elsewhere; but, whether we con-sider the illustrious Body in its own constitution, or in its rules for instruction and direction, we see that it is its very genius to prefer this most excellent prudence to every other gift, and to think little of poetry and of science, unless they happen to be useful.

"It is true that, in the long catalogue of its members, there are to be found the names of the most consumate theologians, and of scholars, the most elegant and accomplished; but we are speaking here, not of individuals, but of the body itself. It is plain that the body is not over-jealous about its theological traditions, or it certainly would not suffer Suarez to controvert with Molina, Viva with Vasquez, Passaglia with Petavius, and

Faure with Suarez, de Lugo, and Valentia. In this intellectual freedom its members justly glory; inasmuch as they have set their affections, not on the opinions of the Schools, but on the souls of men. And it is the same charitable motive which makes them give up the poetry of life, the poetry of ceremonies — of the cowl, the cloister, and the choir — content with the most prosaic architecture, if it be but convenient, and the most prosaic neighborhood, if it be but populous."

Newman was always generous in his praise of the Society. I cannot resist the temptation of quoting the last sentence in this part of his essay where he ascribes to the three Orders the characteristics of three Patriarchs in the Old Testament, drawing an analogy between the Society and the Patriarch Jacob, "the persecuted and helpless, visited by marvellous providences, driven from place to place, set down and taken up again, ill-treated by those who were his debtors, suspected because of his sagacity, and betrayed by his eager faith, yet carried on and triumphing amid all troubles by means of his most faithful and powerful guardian-archangel."

Newman, it can be seen, did not believe that the Society concentrates its best efforts on the production of what we may be allowed to call star performers. His opinion was much the same as that of Father Gerard Manley Hopkins. In the letter, dated December 1, 1881, in *The Correspondence of Gerard Manley Hopkins and Richard Watson Dixon* (Oxford University Press), we find Hopkins, who had then been a Jesuit for thirteen years, writing as follows to the Anglican Canon: "Our Society values, as you say, and has contributed to literature, to culture; but only as a means to an end. Its history and its experience shew that literature proper, as poetry, has seldom been found to be to that end a very serviceable means. We have had for three centuries often the flower of the youth of a country in numbers enter our body: among these how many poets, how many artists of all sorts, there must have been. But there have been very few Jesuit poets and, where they have been, I believe it would be found on examination that there was something exceptional in their circumstances or, so to say, counterbalancing in their career. For genius attracts fame and individual fame St. Ignatius looked on as the most dangerous and dazzling of all attractions. There was a certain Father Beschi who in Southern Hindustan composed an epic which has become one of the Tamul classics and is spoken of with unbounded admiration by those who can read it. But this was in India, far from home, and one can well understand that fame among Hindu pundits need not turn the head of an Italian. In England we had Father Southwell a poet, a minor poet but still a poet; but he wrote amidst a terrible persecution and died a martyr, with circumstances of horrible barbarity: this is the counterpoise in his career. Then what a genius was Campion himself! Was not he a poet? Perhaps a great one, if he had chosen. His *History of Ireland,* written in hiding and hurrying from place to place, Mr. Simpson in his Life says, and the samples prove it, shews an eloquence like Shakespeare's; and in fact Shakespeare made use of the book. He had all and more than all the rhetoric of that golden age and was probably the most vigorous mind and eloquent tongue engaged in theological strife then in England, perhaps in Europe. It seems in time he might have done anything. But his eloquence died on the air, his genius was quenched in his blood after one year's employment in his country.

"Music is more professional than poetry perhaps, and Jesuits have composed and well, but none has any fame to speak of. We had one painter who reached excellence, I forget his name, he was a laybrother; but then he only painted flower pieces. You see then what is against me, but since, as Solomon says, there is a time for everything, there is nothing that does not some day come to be, it may be that the time will come for my verses. I remember, by the by, once taking up a little book of the life of St. Stanislaus told or commented on under emblems; it was much in the style of Herbert and his school and about that date; it was by some Polish Jesuit. I was astonished at their beauty and brilliancy, but the author is quite obscure. Brilliancy does not suit us. Bourdaloue is reckoned our greatest orator: he is severe in style. Suarez is our most famous theologian: he is a man of vast volume of mind, but without originality and brilliancy; he treats everything satisfactorily, but you never remember a phrase of his, the manner is nothing. Molina is the man who *made* our theology: he was a genius and even in his driest dialectic I have remarked a certain fervor like a poet's. But in the great controversy on the Aids of Grace, the most dangerous crisis, as I suppose, which our Society ever went through till its suppression, though it was from his book that it had risen, he took, I think, little part.

"The same sort of thing may be noticed in our saints. St. Ignatius himself was certainly, everyone who reads his life will allow, one of the most extraordinary men that ever lived; but after the establishment of the Order he lived in Rome so ordinary, so hidden, a life, that when after his death they began to move in the process of his canonization, one of the Cardinals, who had known him in his later life and in that way only, said that he had never remarked anything in him more than in any edifying priest. St. Stanislaus Kostka's life and vocation is a bright romance — till he entered the noviceship, where after ten months he died — and at the same time its interest ceases. Much the same may be said of St. Aloysius Gonzaga. The Blessed John Berchmans was beatified [canonized in 1888] for his most exact observance of the rule; he said of himself and the text is famous among us, 'Common life is the greatest of my mortifications'; Gregory XVI (I think) when the first steps were to be taken said of him too: At that rate you will have to canonize all the Roman College. I quote these cases to prove that show and brilliancy do not suit us, that we cultivate the commonplace outwardly and wish the beauty of the king's daughter the soul to be from within."

A false notion may easily be formed from what has been said and quoted here. It is not quite true to say that show and brilliancy do not suit the Society, in the sense that it does not wish its members, as opportunity and occasion offer, to be impressively competent. The Society sets aside men for special studies in which they seem to have an aptitude, and it expects them to be able to give a good account of themselves when called upon. It does this, it is true, when it can release the men from pressing engagements of the hour. Father Hopkins, for instance, would probably have a better chance of cultivating literature today than he had more than fifty years ago when his Province was less numerous and the demands upon its missionary resources greater. The persecutions, which have curtailed the active ministry of Jesuits so often in some European countries, were useful in one respect: they left more Jesuits free to devote themselves to study. This may partially explain why it is that Jesuits in those countries have acquired a greater reputation for scholarship than their brothers in other lands where the urgency of religious work coincided with freedom to satisfy it. Newman is right in saying that the Society has a practical and immediate work to do and goes about it in a practical way. A Jesuit may, like Carlyle, loathe schoolmastering; but, if he has the spirit of his Order, he will take up and pursue schoolmastering with enthusiasm. His special aptitude may help him even on uncongenial ground, while a definite and daily task may have a stabilizing influence on whatever exercise of his special talent he may find the leisure for. Carlyle might have been less erratic and fantastic if he had maintained a regular and practical contact with everyday realities of a homely kind.

There is generally enough free time in a Jesuit's life for the private cultivation of a particular aptitude if the aptitude is strong enough to snatch at odd moments. It is something that works its way up through the toughest soil and needs little or no encouragement. It is interesting to watch that of Father

Hopkins asserting itself in the face of the elements as it were. And it is still more interesting to observe that life in the Society gave the exercise of his aptitude a seriousness and balance which it would conceivably have missed if there were nothing else to occupy his thoughts. Father Hopkins had a full schedule of duties which he was scrupulously conscientious in following. But he used odds and ends of time to become a notable poet and a literary critic of the first importance.

René Fülöp-Miller scornfully dismisses Jesuits as incompetent literary critics because they approach art and poetry from the moral side. It is not a bad way to approach them if, as Walter Pater pointed out, we are looking for great art and not for the trivial kind. Hopkins is an excellent example of how a profound knowledge and reverence for moral standards can enrich and give depth to literary criticism. In an impressionistic world of fluctuating principles a Jesuit critic enjoys special advantages. It is too much to expect of a Jesuit that he wax enthusiastic over a piece, no matter how skillfully done, that, mistakenly or not, deliberately or unintentionally, at least is, objectively, a grave sin against the Creator and an inducement to sin for admiring readers. It involves a false conception of life. A thing of beauty is a joy forever in an ideal world. But, as we find ourselves in a world like this — with Matthew Arnold's "average sensual man" surviving all the modern agencies of refinement — the pursuit of beauty tends to degenerate into commonplace sensuality. "If the modern world," says Chesterton, "will not insist on having some sharp and definite moral law, capable of resisting the counter-attractions of art and humor, the modern world will simply be given over as a spoil to anybody who can manage to do a nasty thing in a nice way. Every murderer who can murder entertainingly will be allowed to murder."

Newman has left us a graphic description of the spiritual and religious dangers attending intellectual employments in his sermon on "Intellect the Instrument of Religious Training," which he preached before the Catholic University in Dublin on the Feast of St. Monica. I think the prayer with which he closes his sermon is a very complete expression of the way the Society wishes its members to engage in intellectual work: "Look down then upon us from Heaven, O Blessed Monica, for we are engaged in supplying that very want which called for thy prayers, and gained for thee thy crown. Thou who didst obtain thy son's conversion by the merit of thy intercession, continue that intercession for us, that we may be blest, as human instruments, in the use of those human means by which ordinarily the Holy Cross is raised aloft, and religion commands the world. Gain for us, first, that we may intensely feel that God's grace is all in all, and that we are nothing; next, that, for His greater glory, and for the honor of Holy Church, and for the good of man, we may be 'zealous for the better gifts,' and may excel in intellect as we excel in virtue."

CHAPTER 24

THE OLD SOCIETY AND THE NEW

THE "Spiritual Exercises" ends with eighteen "Rules for Thinking with the Church." The twelfth rule reads: "We ought to guard against making comparisons between the living and the blessed who have passed away; for no slight error is committed in saying, for example, He knows more than St. Austin; he is as great as, or greater than, St. Francis; he is another St. Paul in holiness and virtue, etc."

Undoubtedly comparisons with the great dead, in a generous impulse to exalt the living, are futile and often foolish. They are futile because, when they are made, they cannot be proved or disproved; and their folly often begins to appear as soon as the enthusiasm of the moment wanes. It is a common occurrence in the history of literature. Some author of the day is hailed by his contemporaries as another Milton or another Dickens to the derisive amusement of the next generation of critics. In the words of St. Ignatius, "no slight error is committed" in the drawing of wild comparisons.

I am not going to expose myself to this error. Within the Society, living Jesuits look back at the men and achievements of the Old Society with reverent admiration, much in the spirit, I fancy, of an historic army regiment which regards with affectionate pride its heroes of the past who established an honorable tradition and set a noble standard of performance. Officers and men are ready to acknowledge their inferiority to the men of old. Their sense of inferiority is a tribute to their heroes of renown; it is not a weak resignation to lower standards of honor and courage nor a defeatest frame of mind. Their moderate opinion of their own worth is precisely the measure of their inspiration in emulating their regimental ancestors whenever the test confronts them.

This chapter would not be written were it not for the charge sometimes made that the Society, since its restoration in 1814, forty years after its suppression, has not recovered its former spirit, being notably behind the Old Society in eminent men and achievements. Superficially, this looks like a serious charge with considerable foundation. One must admit that, if the New Society has the same spirit as of old, this spirit should be manifesting itself outwardly as it always did. I maintain that it does; and I do so without feeling it necessary to declare that modern Jesuits can equal their former brothers in a comparative study of individual eminence. In a Society, which does not make individual eminence, except in sanctity, a primary end of its existence, a tally of eminent men outside the roster of saints is not a reliable way of arriving at conclusions about its spirit. The modern Jesuit draws his inspiration from the same sources as always, from the "Spiritual Exercises" and the Constitutions of his Order: and there is nothing in them about any individual eminence. Even when spiritual eminence in serving God is the only eminence urged upon the members of the Society, it is not conceived as eminence in the common acceptance of that word, something that is calculated to win popular approval and admiration. Spiritual eminence is a secret of the heart, and its unavoidable disclosure generally elicits anything but applause from a contemporary world.

Still, it remains true that, even if eminence is secondary and incidental in the Society, it should be observeable in the modern Society as a sign of its continuity in the spirit and tradition of its founding fathers. And I think it will be generally acknowledged by dispassionate readers that in modern times eminence has been sufficiently noteworthy in the sons to establish the claim of paternity. They have been eminent in dogmatic and moral theology, scholastic philosophy, canon law, Biblical exegesis, archeology, ecclesiastical history, mystical theology, in all studies closely connected with the life of the Church. As for literature and the natural sciences, they have been accomplished and learned enough to be in the first ranks of those who oppose the adversaries of religion; and they have at times extorted the admiration as well as the respect of their enemies.

I do not wish to be boastful. I am ready to agree that the Church has contained men who have been and are more eminent than individual Jesuits. And I can also agree with those who assert that eminence in the New Society has not been so conspicuously distinguished as in the Old. But I venture to believe that eminence is a family trait of the modern Society, as much as formerly, if not in degree at least in kind.

The real eminence, which the Society values as essential, is the holiness and perfection of its members. If it fails of eminence here, it might well be a reproach to its fathers. If it is faithful to the "Spiritual Exercises" and to the Constitutions, it should be still making saints. And here we are on ground which it is hard to traverse. I shall be the first to agree that every Jesuit is not a saint; I know at least one who is not. About others I cannot say, since sanctity is not always worn on the sleeve. But I have met in my limited experience Jesuits who looked very much like saints, so much so that I would not be at all surprised if I were told that their causes would be submitted to Rome for ultimate canonization. There are about thirty modern Jesuits who have passed the first stages of official scrutiny on the way to canonization; and some thirty others whose causes are going through the preliminary processes. Canonization is not a hasty business. Some Jesuit saints who lived three hundred years ago have been canonized in my own lifetime. Any discussion of the way the Society has been living up to its tradition must be postponed a couple of centuries if we are to insist upon the conclusive proof of canonization.

If every Jesuit is not a saint, it is not the fault of the Society, which continues to give him the same spiritual food that made saints in the past. And here we come upon another criticism launched against the New Society. It is said that the Society, after all, is only a human institution and that it is the common fate of all human institutions to flourish for a while and then to enter a period of gradual decay until they become moribund. This is an antecedent judgment only; but it rests on a principle which everyone accepts as sound. As applied to the Society, with the inference that the modern Society cannot have un-diminished the spirit of the Old, it is a judgment which the Society keeps in mind as a warning against laxity. It is to be remembered, too, that a human institution inside the Church is not so subject to the law of mortality as a secular institution. Religious Orders share in a measure the immortality of the Church. They may need reform in the course of centuries: the Church can take care of that.

As time is measured in the Church, four hundred years do do not constitute a very long span. The revival of the Society, after the social and political cataclysm at the end of the eight-eenth century, can be regarded in a certain sense as a rebirth of the Society. It resumed its full life with rejuvenated vigor and a holy ambition to continue its ancient traditions. In this respect, it may be supposed to have at present the energy and eagerness of youth.

Moreover, the government of the Society in modern times is carried on in conditions more favorable to its unity and the preservation of its spirit than at any time in the past. "In large bodies," declared Edmund Burke at the time of the American Revolution, "the circulation of power must be less rigorous at the extremities. . . . There must be a prudent relaxation in all the borders. This is the immutable condition, the eternal law, of extensive and detached empire." The practical wisdom, which Burke here expressed in the case of a government with remote dependencies, has a certain amount of applicability to any ecclesiastical body whose provinces cover the globe. But the need of moderation on the distant fringes of jurisdiction always carries with it a menace to unity and loyalty.

Never in the history of the Society has this menace had less chance to arise than now. Cable and telephone, radio and rapid postal service and swift transportation, have brought men and places, geographically distant, into comparative neighborhood. The Society of Jesus in Australia and North and South America, the 3,500 Jesuits in Madagascar, Nanking, Patna, Alaska, Mangalore, Zambesi, British Honduras and British Guiana, Bosnia and Bagdad, to mention at random a few of the scenes of Jesuit missionary labors, are in normal circumstances and in terms of communication hardly more than a few weeks distant at the remotest stations from the central seat of authority in Rome. It is almost inconceivable, for example, that a situation could be permitted to develop anywhere in the Society similar to that which arose in Portugal in the Generalship of St. Ignatius himself, when, on account of poor communication and the loose control of Father Rodriguez, the Society had come to such a pass that 213 members had to be summarily dismissed. If laxity begin to creep into the Society at present, it will not be for unavoidable defects in its machinery of government.

It is in the field of education especially that the modern Jesuits are sometimes said to be conspicuously inferior to their brethren of old. Their schools do not enjoy the same reputation of undisputed excellence as formerly. In examining the justice of this criticism, I would first call attention to the historical fact that the Society was not founded to be an educational Order. The education of youth was, so to speak, an afterthought of St. Ignatius. His sole purpose at the start was to promote the cause of religion. As the young Order grew, it was seen that the work of education was a powerful instrument in the fulfillment of his purpose and from that time on the resources of the Order were drawn on heavily to man schools and colleges. I call attention to this fact in order to point out that, even if the schools of the Society were superseded in modern times by better Catholic schools, the loss would not necessarily imply a falling away from the spirit of its founder. It took up the work of education for the glory of God and religion, and, if others can now be found to do that work more efficiently, it is content to turn to something else.

The Society, however, is still actively engaged in education. Is it true that its schools have everywhere lost their ancient prestige? In conducting schools of a purely ecclesiastical kind, it is not, I venture to say, going too far to assert that Jesuits are upholding their inherited tradition. As for schools of secular education for the laity, it may be admitted that they have not had in modern times any replicas of Collége Louis-le-Grand or La Flèche. But it would indicate a rather serious defect of historical information to lay this deficiency at the door of the Jesuits. The schools of the modern Society have had to undergo unprecedented vicissitudes in most of the European countries. There has been hardly time for a Jesuit institution of learning to be well started before some new form of government has come along to suppress it. It is not an uncommon experience of travellers in so-called Catholic countries to be told that this government building or that was once a Jesuit college. As for those non-Catholic countries where Jesuit activity in education has some measure of freedom, there is a notable lack of the rich patrons without whom the arts and sciences, pursued for their own sake and not for profit, find it difficult to flourish with dazzling success.

In this country the Jesuits have been reproached for departing from the spirit of their forefathers in paying less attention than formerly to classical studies. It needs only a slight knowledge of the history of modern education to be aware that no change of spirit was involved. That popular and shallow thinker, Thomas Huxley, and the utilitarian theorists of the past century, advocated the replacement of the classics by the natural sciences as an instrument of education in terms which the masses could understand. The obvious usefulness of scientific studies to the individual and the State in a grossly material world was an argument less subtle and far more comprehensible to the average mind than any that could be brought to bear in favor of the classics. A growing enthusiasm for utilitarian education became irresistible. Men like Cardinal Newman and Matthew Arnold strove vainly to stem the tide. I think the Jesuits were among the last to succumb to a popular demand that was being enforced by State Boards and powerful standardizing agencies. While Jesuits favor the classics, they do not favor them to the extent of sacrificing their main purpose of engaging in educational work for the good of religion. If students would not attend classical schools, the rational step was to conduct schools which they would attend. In 1938 the Jesuits had in the United States 33 high schools with an attendance of nearly 15,000; and 23 colleges and universities with 43,000 students.

The Jesuits have a working tradition in education which lends a distinctive impress to their schools whatever be the courses. This impress, no doubt, is partly due to scholastic philosophy which has always been retained and still remains an important part of the curriculum. It is conceivable that the modern revival of interest in scholasticism owes some of its success to the persistent attention and high place always accorded this branch of learning in Jesuit schools.

Whenever circumstances were favorable to the classical tradition, modern Jesuits have carried on as of old. In his autobiography, published by the Columbia University Press in 1938, with a foreword by Nicholas Murray Butler, Friedrich Paulsen, the noted German educator and philosopher, tells how he incurred the wrath of his associates for praising the Jesuits in his *History of Higher Education in German Schools and Universities.*

"I was violently attacked because of my unprejudiced appreciation of the Jesuits' schools and chided for my lack of

Protestant spirit: I became known as 'the Janssen of the history of education.' The unforgiveable sin I had committed consisted in having proved by documentary evidence that the decline of the schools and universities in the third decade of the sixteenth century was one of the first and most immediate consequences of the Reformation."

A few pages later on he describes a visit he paid to the Jesuit classical school at Feldkirch in Austria. There were no Jesuit schools in Germany, having been banned by Bismark.

"It was the most magnificent and best equipped establishment of the boarding-school type I had ever seen. The classrooms, the dormitories and dining rooms, the church and the great hall were all equipped for sturdy efficiency, but not without elegance or a sense of beauty. The impressive library was well stocked with modern scientific works, and my *History of Higher Education* was also in evidence. A beautiful large garden with playgrounds and recreational facilities of every sort provided an appropriate setting. . . . Most of the pupils came from the German Empire, especially from its Catholic western provinces; there were several scions of noble families among them. . . . A few years later I found things just the same on the Freinberg near Linz."

These two schools, together with the other Jesuit schools in Austria, were suppressed in the recent *Anschluss* of Mr. Hitler, and now there are in Europe several more government buildings that used to be Jesuit colleges. The New Society has, at least, that much in common with the Old, it is still the first to feel the displeasure of the enemies of religion.

The following extract from Father Philip Hughes's article on "Pius the Eleventh" in the *Dublin Review* for April, 1939, encourages Jesuits to believe that the family likeness has not been wholly lost in the corrosive processes of time. Father Hughes is not a Jesuit, and, as far as available records show, never had Jesuit teachers. He writes like a detached observer.

"The known affection of Pius XI for the Society, the succes-

sion of important Catholic works he committed to its members,
like the known preference for his own *Milanese,* had much
more than personal preference behind it. Tasks needed doing
and the Pope wanted to be assured that there would always
be men competent for the work, and that these could somehow be rapidly mobilized. And in the Society of Jesus he
found a whole corps of specialists who could adapt themselves,
technicians prepared at a moment's notice to fill gaps and, if
need be, spend their lives filling gaps. This is an idealized
picture of Jesuit efficiency, and Jesuits who read this will be
the first to smile at it. But, it seems to me, there is sufficient
truth in it to show why Pope Pius XI, whose own spirit was
so akin to that of the Society, so readily turned, in his simple
direct desire that a job should be done now and done once
and for all — and never turned in vain — to the Jesuit General
for the handyman he needed. Sometimes it was a new Institute of Higher Studies for which a staff must rapidly be found,
sometimes a hundred typists who understood Latin to copy
documents, where lack of copies was delaying the progress of
a *causa beatificationis.* The Pope soon came to him in all
emergencies as to one sure source, to the man who never was
not able, and so to the exasperation of a few, and to no doubt
mingled amusement and dismay of those most intimately
concerned, the papal-Jesuit co-operation became a feature of
the pontificate."

The saintly founder of the Society, I think, would read this
testimony about his sons with pleasure, seeing in it evidence
that his spirit still lived in them. The only thing that could
spoil and nullify it in his eyes would be any indication that
the Jesuits, found so useful by a great pope, were concerned
about their individual reputations or thought more of the interests of the Society than of the glory of God and the welfare
of the Church.

CHAPTER 25

FATHER HOPKINS AND THE SOCIETY

A MAJOR poet can turn up anywhere; being a genius he is not the product of special training or a particular kind of environment. Due regard for this general law might have saved certain writers from an embarrassing position. After a profound study of the Society of Jesus, they all agreed that, whatever its merits, it could not produce a great poet. And then suddenly Gerard Manley Hopkins was sprung upon them by leading literary critics as a major poet of the nineteenth century, some going so far as to assert that he was its greatest poet. Whether these claims will stand the only test, that of time, no one can say. Prophecy is hazardous.

The Jesuits, however, were not allowed to enjoy a triumph over the prophets. In the nature of things, the prophets should be embarrassed. But, as the facts are represented now, it is the Jesuits who should be embarrassed. Why did they receive the young poet into their Society? As if he were the usual average grist for their mill. Why did they allow him to bury his genius in the pursuit of their strange spiritual ideals? Why for so many years did they subject him to the common discipline and burden him with occupations of a dray-horse kind? Why did they never accord him the recognition he deserved? And so on, and so on. The Jesuits ought to hide their diminished heads. If it were not for Robert Bridges and others who salvaged the wreckage from Jesuit backwaters, few would have heard of Hopkins. Thus we arrive at an interesting conclusion. If the Jesuits produce no poet, they are scorned. And, if they produce a poet, they are scorned. You would think Hopkins was a Jesuit asset: he turns out to be a Jesuit liability. This is a crazy world.

Yet, not so crazy as it seems. Whatever a Jesuit here or there may think, the Society of Jesus as a whole is not seriously concerned as to whether Hopkins is or is not a major poet. When Hopkins, with the encouragement of Cardinal Newman, entered the Society, he did so on the understanding that it would help him to be a better man. If it had tried instead to make him a better poet, Hopkins would have been disappointed, and the Society would have been practising that duplicity for which it is famous among its detractors. It may be a horrible thing to say, but the Society does not agree at all with those bright people who think that a poet should be a poet first and always even if it involves declension to a lower plane of moral effort.

The respective claims of natural genius and personal perfection is an interesting topic that comes up again and again in the three enthralling volumes of *Letters,* and *Note-Books and Papers,* of Gerard Manley Hopkins, published by the Oxford University Press. In one of the letters addressed to Bridges, Hopkins states the case in favor of sanctity; under a thin disguise, it is true, but clearly. The disguise was necessary on account of the distaste which Bridges always felt for religious discussion. Bridges was a good man of a low-power kind. He liked his own ideas of religion so much that he resented enlightenment from any Church but especially the Catholic Church; constitutionally incapable, it appears, of casting off the traditional middle-class dislike of Catholics so strong in England. Hopkins loved him, and every now and then, rather pathetically, did a little fishing for him. This was the sort of man for whom Hopkins tried to establish the superior claims of personal perfection over genius.

"I quite understand what you mean about gentlemen and 'damfools'; it is a very striking thing, and I could say more on the subject. I shall not say that much, but I say this: if a gentleman feels that to be what we call a gentleman is a thing essentially higher than, without being a gentleman, to be ever so great an artist or thinker; or if, to put it another way, an artist or thinker feels that, were he to become in those ways ever so great, he would still essentially be lower than a gentleman that was no artist and no thinker — then how much more must art and philosophy and manners and breeding and everything else in the world be below the least degree of true virtue. This is that chastity of mind which seems to lie at the very heart and be the parent of all other good, the seeing at once what is best, the holding to that, and the not allowing anything else whatever to be even heard pleading to the contrary.

"Christ's life and character are such as appeal to all the world's admiration, but there is one insight St. Paul gives us of it which is very secret and seems to me more touching and constraining than everything else is: This mind, he says, was in Christ Jesus — he means as man: being in the form of God — that is, finding, as in the first instant of his incarnation he did, his human nature informed by the godhead — he thought it nevertheless no snatching-matter for him to be equal with God, but annihilated himself, taking the form of servant; that is, he could not but see what he was, God, but he would see it as if he did not see it, and be it as if he were not, and, instead of snatching at once at what all the time was his, or was himself, he emptied or exhausted himself, so far as that was possible, of godhead and behaved only as God's slave, as His creature, as man, which also he was, and then being in the guise of man humbled himself to death, the death of the cross.

"It is this holding of himself back, and not snatching at the truest and highest good, the good that was his right, nay his possession from a past eternity in his other nature, his own being and self, which seems to me the root of all moral good in other men. I agree then, and vehemently, that a gentleman, if there is such a thing on earth, is in a position to despise the poet, were he Dante or Shakespeare, and the painter, were he

Angelo or Apelles, for anything in him that showed him *not* to be a gentleman. He is in the position to do it, I say, but if he is a gentleman perhaps that is what he will not do. . . . As a fact poets and men of art, are, I am sorry to say, by no means necessarily or commonly gentlemen. For gentlemen do not pander to lust or other basenesses nor, as you say, give themselves airs and affectations nor do other things to be found in modern works."

This is a good treatise, in miniature, on spiritual perfection, written for a friend whose obtuseness to the supernatural was always a trial to Hopkins. The future author of *The Testament of Beauty* was never a profound philosopher. A good man, and in a large measure unworldly, he never could rise above the material-minded and commonplace views of his world concerning the religious life of the Catholic Church. To the end he wept over the "housecarl in Loyola's menie." The little treatise on perfection had no effect. But we cannot blame a blind man for not seeing: and, as Louise Imogen Guiney put it, his devotion to the memory of his Jesuit friend makes him forever "thanksworthy."

Did the Society of Jesus afford Hopkins the opportunities for spiritual growth that he expected? And did he take advantage of them? The answer to both questions can, I think, be found in the published letters. It is curious to observe in them how Hopkins naturally and unconsciously assumes an intellectual superiority which his correspondents never resent and seem to expect. But it is still more curious to observe how they recognize in him a moral superiority also. Since Bridges destroyed his own letters to Hopkins, we can only infer this recognition from the replies to them. But in Canon Dixon's letters, there is occasionally something of that awe which is the common tribute we pay to sanctity. Everywhere throughout these letters we have the picture of a man whose mind is fixed on spiritual ends, not without valor in the pursuit of them. The picture is not direct portraiture; rather the general effect of faint hints and chance phrases and the apparently thoughtless gestures which disclose the soul. Whatever be the verdict ultimately pronounced upon the poems, the letters bear unmistakable evidence of a strong man striving, often painfully, after that perfection which his chosen vocation encouraged; we are here on high grounds where art values are secondary and rather insignificant .

An intimate friend of Father Hopkins in his last years declared:

"I think the characteristics in him that most struck and edified all of us who knew him were, first, what I should call his priestly spirit; this showed itself not only in the reverential way he performed his sacred duties and spoke on sacred subjects, but in his whole conduct and conversation; and, secondly, his devotion and loyalty to the Society of Jesus."

Stevenson uttered a truism when he said that life is not designed to minister to a man's vanity. Least of all does it do so in a Religious Order. And, from every point of view, this is as it should be. Whenever life happens to encourage a man's vanity, the result is usually rather appalling, more spiritually disastrous probably than the rebellious resentment of the weaker sort who are broken by life's humiliations. In the Religious life a man may react in many ways to the assaults upon his vanity. He may give up and go back to the world, honestly acknowledging his incompetence; or his hurt vanity may make him gradually forget the supernatural character of his life and fill him with grievances against Superiors and rules, so that, when he reaches the term of endurance, he leaves the Order, cursing the life and everything in it.

The natural disposition and artist temper of Father Hopkins found their own difficulties in Jesuit life; but it must be apparent to every reader of the poems and letters that, if the Society tried him, it also supported him in his trials. The Society for him was the minister of a loving Providence; its rules and Superiors were the purveyors of God's will; he put himself in their hands with a trust that never faltered, that was as wholehearted after twenty years as it was in his novice days, and, for all the "terrible sonnets" and disheartening failures, never once regretted.

Those who dwell upon Father Hopkins' dark hours, as if he were a gentle victim on the Jesuit rack, are usually the kind of people who speak of the religious life as a weak man's refuge from trouble. They can blow hot or cold to suit their purpose. The world has its own troubles, and so has the Religious life. We need not stop to compare them. But it may pertinently be observed that anyone who seriously sets himself the task of advancing in spiritual perfection has about as big a job to tackle as any that life in the world can offer.

The sequel of fame that came belatedly to Father Hopkins is as startling as anything to be encountered in the pages of hagiography — which is always startling. When Canon Dixon urged him to take some steps toward the publication of his poems, he declined on the score that, if Providence wished it, his Superiors would act in the matter. He would not obtrude his will. He left the publication of his poems entirely to Providence. Poetry was a minor care with Father Hopkins; but one of the most refreshing features in the chronicles of sanctity is the way Omnipotence attends to little things — like the catching of fishes in a net or the multiplication of loaves of bread. No one can deny that Providence did handsomely by the poems of Gerard Manley Hopkins.

CHAPTER 26

INDIVIDUALITY AND RULES

I HAVE often been puzzled by a certain clairvoyant faculty of discernment which nearly everybody seems to possess except me. It is common to hear people boast that they can tell a priest no matter how secularly he may be disguised. They sometimes go further and claim they can tell a Benedictine or a Dominican or a Redemptorist or a Passionist, and so on, even when he is clad in ordinary clerical street clothes. The people who interest me particularly, of course, are the people who say they can recognize a Jesuit whenever and wherever they see him.

It is more than I can do after a long lifetime spent among Jesuits. I recall the day I met two clergymen in a street car and fell to chatting with them. To satisfy a mild curiosity and to fill a pause, I asked them in my best company manner what parishes they were attached to. They replied that they were Jesuits and belonged to the same community as myself. It was somewhat embarrassing. I must add by way of extenuation that it was a numerous community lodged in a group of houses. That rather disturbing experience has recurred in modified forms several times since, so that now I approach a strange clergyman with great caution.

This ineptitude on my part makes the keenness of those who say they can tell a Jesuit at sight all the more baffling. I have tried to save myself by allowing largely for the human tendency to exaggerate. But my own experience is on their side. I have frequently been picked out for a Jesuit by total strangers. Once I was looking for a certain street in New York, whither I had just come from a remote province, when a man approached me with an offer to help. After giving me the desired information, he asked me if I were not a Jesuit. I begged him to tell me how he knew. *Incessu patuit Jesuita:* something or other about me, he could not say what. The only clue he could venture was that his brother was a Jesuit.

The most startling instance of this kind that I remember occurred in Stratford-on-Avon where a fellow Jesuit and I were stopping for a day, like good Americans, to pay our respects at the shrine of Shakespeare. We had taken our luncheon at one of the tourist hotels in the town, and were settling with the clerk at the desk, when he electrified us by asking casually if we were Jesuits. For the English Midlands are not much more Catholic than Sweden or Norway, or backward counties in our own country, the last place in the world where a Jesuit could expect to be recognized. We plied the man with all kinds of questions to find out how he could possibly have spotted us. It was no use. The only thing he had to offer that looked like an explanation was the fact that he had worked in the Jesuit house at Manchester when Father Bernard Vaughan was there. As neither of us had anything resembling or faintly suggesting the baronial port of Father Vaughan, we went away unsatisfied.

These are trivial incidents, but they seem to lend color to a rather grave charge against the Jesuits; namely, that they are reduced to a dead level of uniformity by their life and rules, depersonalized, so to say, made into machines with the factory stamp on them. Years ago a college youth in one of my classes repeated this patter to me, having been listening to his elders, or having picked it up in some author who knew all about Jesuits, like Alexander Dumas or Eugene Sue. I was rather appalled at my helplessness to make a suitable reply. What is to be said when you are told that you lack individuality? The school was swarming with Jesuits, no two of whom were alike. It was a case of the tyranny of the press over mind and experience; a very nice instance of antecedent reasoning triumphing over the obvious facts. We all observed the same rules, and therefore we must be the same in character, disposition, inclinations, and whatever else makes a man a distinct individual: we simply must be the same, all facts to the contrary notwithstanding. Besides everybody said so. The only response that occurred to me at the time was that all the Jesuits in that college ate the same meals with noticeably varying results: a fact which the boy could not possibly blink.

Still, the fact remains, apparently equally unblinking, that a hallmark can be recognized by total strangers. It is, as I have said, a mystery to me: I cannot imagine how they do it, and they cannot tell me the secret. But I do not think it is because we have been drilled into a standardized and goose-stepping sameness. It is true that Cardinal Newman said: "All Jesuits have the same cut about them." But I am sure the pleasantry was not intended to be disparaging since he always admired the Jesuits and encouraged Gerard Manley Hopkins to become one. He was just the man to find intolerable a set of men whose rules tended to erase their personality.

The fool in the old Greek story, who was out to sell his house, carried a brick from it around with him as a sample to show prospective buyers: he could not take the house with him on his rounds. There is only a very thin partition between the fool's folly and a rather profound truth. Most of us carry, not our house, but our home with us wherever we go. Every man, woman, and child is a living hint of the homes they come from. The idea will bear expansion, it seems to me, to include not only the family but every body of men who, for any notable period of time, live a common life that is regulated by definite rules and traditions. It is conceivable that such persons by living together acquire a sort of family likeness such as Ovid described, a sameness marked by differences. At least, we hear people declare that they can tell an Oxford man anywhere, or an English public-school man. Harvard, in the same way, is said to leave a mark on its young men.

I do not think this visible mold of form is usually taken to mean that all peculiar traits of the natural character are crushed and rubbed off till the subject has been subdued to a uniform color and type. On the contrary, I believe the impress of a distinguished school is worn with an air and is regarded with favor by people at large. If it is not mere snobbery and is really the effect of training in an atmosphere of noble tradition, everyone will so regard it except, of course, believers in the unbridled individualism of a menagerie. Most of us are rough enough to need a little retouching.

While it is true, as I have said several times already, that I have not the dimmest notion of how one can tell a Jesuit, I cannot bring myself to believe that it is the absence of all individuality. Living among Jesuits intimately, I am almost tempted to say that I see nothing else. I do not deny that they may bear a common mark distinguishable to others. If we have not spent some time in China, it is ordinarily difficult to tell one Chinese from another; but, since the difficulty does not exist among the Chinese themselves, it does not argue the absence of strong personal traits of character. The Chinese, it is said, have the same difficulty with us: to them all Westerners are alike and hard to tell apart. To one looking from the outside, all Jesuits may "have the same cut about them." It is certain that from the inside they present a rather heterogeneous group — in appearance, character, disposition, deportment. To me it will, I fear, always be a mystery how they can be related to some formula by which a stranger can know them — unless it be true of Jesuits, as has been said in another connection, that the more they differ the more they are alike.

By way of parenthesis, I wish to say that I am glad that at various times in their history Jesuits were not so easily recognized as they seem to be today. Otherwise the English priest-hunters would not have had such great trouble in rounding them up for Tyburn and the torture chamber. It was an English grievance at the time, and still is in some quarters, that the Jesuits assumed disguises of various sorts: a low game to play on honest Englishmen. In their indignation they said the Jesuits were jesuitical.

I suppose I shall never learn what it is precisely that discloses the Jesuit. I am greatly concerned to know. I am sure it would be to my advantage. I sometimes have a dreadful fear that, after I am discovered and when I ask for the clue, I am not given it lest my feelings be hurt. There may be, after all, any number of ways of telling a Jesuit, more or less haphazard, some of them, perhaps highly fanciful, when the happy guess is a pure accident. I read the following in a recent book: "We were shown around by a charming little friar. Incidentally all Franciscan friars seem to be small. I do not know whether the humility of their founder has imbued them with a delicate kind of physical shrinkage, or whether the Franciscan life does not appeal to men of large stature." I am quite sure that is a poor rule by which to tell Franciscans; it would never apply to Jesuits, some of whom are colossal. Very likely the rule for distinguishing Jesuits might in many cases prove to be equally fanciful.

But, even if it were, I should like to know it; I should probably reap profit from knowing. Thus, if you could tell me afar because I had a furtive and mysterious look, a certain air of conspiracy and intrigue, I would spend the rest of my life cultivating an open and expansive manner like a successful salesman of stocks and bonds. If it were because of a smart and worldly way of conducting myself, I should feel deeply chagrined and would go into retirement till I got rid of it and had acquired some of the demeanor of a serious and religious man. If I were told that I gave myself away by my crafty countenance, I do not know what could be done about it: I might ask for an inside job and never stir out of the house. Of course, if I looked altogether too crafty, my superiors might permit me to consult a plastic surgeon with a view of hiding my naturally crafty soul under a mask of simple honesty. And so on. There is, alas, no way of knowing how many useful hints for my improvement I am missing because people cannot or will not tell me how they know I am a Jesuit. If, however, they said they could tell I was a Jesuit by some fine trait they thought they saw in me, but which I really did not possess (although I ought to possess it), I should feel profoundly rebuked and bend every effort to grow, if it were possible, to the proper stature.

After all is said, the only thing that need concern a Jesuit very much is whether Loyola will recognize him easily as a Jesuit when they meet.

A FAMOUS BOOK

N O JESUIT has published a book nearly so well known and so highly praised as that which the founder of his Order gave the world with the title, "Spiritual Exercises." It is doubtful whether any single book appearing in the last four hundred years has acquired a more widespread reputation and been more vital with undiminishing vigor in its religious influence. It is no exaggeration to say that, if a modern publisher were to issue an edition of the "Spiritual Exercises," and, after the manner of modern publishers, wished to increase the sale of the book by printing and distributing all the laudatory notices of it by popes, churchmen of all degrees, and famous writers of every shade of religious belief and unbelief, during the last four centuries, he would have to do it in a companion volume larger than the original work. Whatever the Jesuit Order did to stem the flood of Protestantism in the sixteenth century was the work of this little book. And yet, like most great books, while it is spoken of a great deal, it is seldom read.

And that may be just as well. It was never intended to be a book for the public at large. Of all the famous books of the world, the "Spiritual Exercises" must be the most disappointing to the casual and curious reader, who picks it up to see what all this hubbub of laudation is about, with the anticipatory thrill of being electrified which we all feel in approaching for the first time a world-renowned masterpiece. It is no book for an idle reader: is no brilliant performance of an author, which you just sit back and enjoy. The reason is that you are the one who is supposed to do the performing. If you are not in the mood to exert yourself, and do not cast off the role of mere spectator, out for a new sensation, you will find the book dull as dishwater, as insignificant and commonplace in reality as it is in outward appearance, and you will be puzzled by all the reverence paid it for so long a time and from so many diverse quarters.

The disappointed reader cannot accuse St. Ignatius of drawing him on by leading him to expect more than is supplied. The little book is not much bigger than a fair-sized pamphlet and can be read in an hour or two. In its very first paragraph, the author states explicitly that the book is a book of exercises: "As to go for a walk or a journey, and to run, are bodily exercises, so is the term of spiritual exercises applied to any method of preparing and disposing the soul to free itself from all inordinate affections, and after it has freed itself from them, to seek and find the will of God concerning the ordering of life for the salvation of one's soul."

I have no doubt there are books on the market which contain directions and give graduated exercises calculated to restore health of body and develop muscular strength; directions and exercises for the patient and for his doctor or trainer. If a man, not particularly concerned about his health or physical prowess, were to buy the book, looking for entertainment or merely wishing to pass the time, he probably would feel much like the literary explorer who has obtained a copy of the "Spiritual Exercises" and proceeds to read it through at a sitting. When a man has no spiritual problems, or does not much care whether he has or not, his interest in St. Ignatius's booklet will be of the mildest sort. Short as it is, he will skip pages and may never have the patience to finish it.

It opens with twenty brief instructions to the exercitant and his director. These preliminary and general remarks, called "Annotations," are intended to indicate the proper and most intelligent approach to the exercises on the part of director and exercitant. Then, after a few lines describing the right philosophical and Christian attitude toward any possible misunderstanding of a truth, St. Ignatius lays down what he calls the first principle and foundation of human life. Seven pages follow, on the way to examine our conscience and on the advantages of a general confession.

All this is only preparing the ground for the exercises proper, which begin with meditations on sin and its punishment. In setting forth the nature of these meditations, the Saint teaches us how they should be made, how we should begin by begging for God's help; and then, in what he calls the first prelude, bringing before the eyes of the imagination a concrete picture embodying the spirit of the meditation. The second prelude is a prayer for grace in the need brought home to us by the meditation. The points of the meditation follow, when we apply to each point the three powers of the soul, the memory, understanding, and will; and, at the end of the hour, close in a colloquy with God (and sometimes with Christ and our Lady asking them to intercede) communing with Him in the mood of the meditation and telling Him our purpose to get closer to Him. In some of the meditations, the points will consist of applications of the five senses, through the imagination, to the subject matter. St. Ignatius gives detailed outlines of only three meditations in the exercises of the First Week. The others are merely indicated and are for the most part repetitions of the three. At the end of the last of the three meditations, he has a note prescribing the number of meditations for one day and the time for making them, allowing for changes in particular cases.

In ten notes that follow, called "Additions," we have minute instructions on the technique to be followed, and four "Notes" supplementary to the "Additions." Standing by itself at the end of the First Week, and introductory to the following Week, is the meditation on the Kingdom of Christ, which is outlined with some fullness.

I have now gone through more than a fourth of the book. To

the merely curious reader, this dry outline of a very dry book will undoubtedly be heavy going. But, if he is looking for information, I do not see how it can be helped. In bringing this description of a famous book to a close, I shall do my best to try his patience as little as possible. In the early chapters of this book an effort has been made to clothe the skeleton with flesh and to show how the Exercises proceed in practice.

The Second Week begins with two meditations, sketched with severe economy of detail, on the Incarnation and the Nativity. St. Ignatius calls these meditations "contemplations," because the mind is less discursively employed in them, being engaged in watching the scenes and episodes presented to it, and intuitively, as it were, absorbing the lessons conveyed through them. Three preludes are used instead of two, the first prelude being to recall "the history of the matter which I have to contemplate," the other two remaining the same as before. There is also a slight change in the manner of the colloquy. Five notes are interjected with fresh instructions suitable to the Second Week. Here, as in previous instructions, St. Ignatius reminds the retreat-master to adapt all instructions to the capacity, mental and physical, of the retreatant. For the second and third days, the subjects of the contemplations are merely indicated. The subject of the last of these contemplations is the Christ Child in the Temple, and a note calls attention to the fact that it presents to the mind the superiority of God's claims upon us above all earthly claims, thus preparing the way for the two Ignatian meditations of the fourth day, "The Two Standards" and the "The Three Classes."

St. Ignatius puts twelve days into his "Second Week," but adds that the Week may be shortened or lengthened, and some of the prescribed contemplations omitted, since the purpose is to teach a method of contemplating which can continue to be used when the retreat is over. After merely setting down subjects from our Lord's public life up to the Passion for the remaining eight days of the Week, the Saint has three notes in which he introduces another subject for serious attention during this Week. On the fifth day, after the contemplation of Christ's departure from Nazareth for the Jordan, the matter of what he calls the Election is to be brought into the retreat. The Election is the choice of a state of life, or of a higher standard of perfection in the life we are following.

It is clear the Saint attaches the greatest importance to this part of the Week's exercises. He devotes eight pages to its discussion. I shall give only the headings of his series of observations: He explains first the three degrees of humility to clarify the nature of the choice that is to be made, and then, under the general heading of Election, treats the subject under the following subheads:

Prelude for Making the Election.

Consideration for the Purpose of Obtaining Knowledge of the Matters About Which an Election is to be Made, Which Contains Four Points and a Note.

Three Times in Which a Good and Right Election May be Made.

The First Method of Making a Good and Right Election Contains Six Points.

The Second Method of Making a Good and Right Election Contains Four Rules and a Note.

To Amend and Reform One's Whole Life and State.

The Third Week is devoted to contemplations on the Passion from the time our Lord left Bethany to "our Lady's arrival at her house, after the Burial of her Son." The incidents are taken in their historical order, so many for each contemplation: an alternative is offered of selecting only the more prominent. The Saint gives an outline for the first contemplation, which has six points. The second prelude, or "composition of place," is characteristic: "It will be here to view the way from Bethany to Jerusalem, whether broad, or narrow, or level, etc., and likewise the supper room, whether great or small, whether of this shape or some other." For the second contemplation, only the three preludes are given. On the seventh day of Week, the whole Passion is reviewed, pondering at times on the separation of Christ's soul and body, and on the sorrowful solitude of our Lady and the disciples. Two more days can be spent in going over the Passion, half of it at a time, and another day in contemplating it again as a whole. The notes for this Week are few: the last two pages contain eight rules for "Regulating Oneself for the Future in the Matter of Food."

The Fourth Week, the last, is the shortest. The opening contemplation, on how our Lord appeared to our Lady, is given and the final one "For Obtaining Love." In between the two, the Saint has four notes of instruction for the exercises of this Week. Then comes a little treatise of less than six small pages on the "Three Methods of Prayer," with the subheads:

> First Method of Prayer.
> > First, On the Ten Commandments.
> > Secondly, On the Deadly Sins.
> > Thirdly, On the Powers of the Soul.
> > Fourthly, On the Five Senses of the Body.
> Second Method of Prayer.
> Third Method of Prayer.

And after this we have twenty-three pages containing matter which we might expect to be placed as an appendix immediately after the Four Weeks. In these pages St. Ignatius has a list of fifty-two subjects for meditation, with the title, "The Mysteries of the Life of Christ Our Lord." He gives a word of introduction: "It is to be noticed that in all the following Mysteries the words in italics are taken from the Gospel itself; but this is not the case with the rest; and in order to facilitate meditation and contemplation on the Mysteries, three points will generally be given for each." The points are given for all but four of the Mysteries. These points are exceedingly short: the Saint always believed that it was better to have the exercitant develop the points for himself. Many of the points are merely brief extracts from the Scripture.

This fidelity to the written Word is characteristic of the "Exercises." Newman refers to it in a passage of the *Apologia,* in which he describes the effect of the "Spiritual Exercises" upon him as he advanced toward Rome. "What I can speak of with greater confidence is the effect upon me a little later of the Exercises of St. Ignatius. Here again, in a pure matter of the most direct religion, in the intercourse between God and the soul, during a season of recollection, of repentance, of good resolution, of inquiry into vocation, the soul was *sola cum solo;* there was no cloud interposed between the creature and the Object of his faith and love. The command practically enforced was, 'My Son, give me thy heart.' The devotions then to angels and saints as little interfered with the incommunicable glory of the Eternal, as the love which we bear our friends and relations, our tender human sympathies, are inconsistent with that supreme homage of the heart to the Unseen, which really does but sanctify and exalt what is of earth."

As an example of the extreme brevity of the points given by St. Ignatius, here is one of these fifty-two meditations:

On the Nativity of Christ Our Lord.
(St. Luke ii. 1–14)

1. Our Lady and her spouse Joseph go from Nazareth to Bethlehem. *"And Joseph went up from Galilee to Bethlehem* to profess subjection to Caesar, *with Mary his espoused wife, who was with child."*

2. *"And she brought forth her first-born Son, and wrapped him up in swaddling clothes and laid him in a manger."*

3. *"There was . . . a multitude of the heavenly army saying: Glory to God in the highest."*

The Saint seldom has recourse to tradition, and, when he has, he is at pains to say so. Thus, in his meditation on the twelfth apparition of our risen Lord, he says Christ "appeared to Joseph

of Arimathea, as may be piously thought, and as we read in the
Lives of the Saints." The next and last apparition, given as a
subject for meditation, is Christ's appearance to St. Paul. The
series of meditations ends with one on the Ascension.

Lastly we have about eighteen pages which many readers
will find the most interesting in the book. The headings will
indicate their nature.

Rules for the Discernment of Spirits.

Rules for in Some Degree Perceiving and Knowing the
Various Motions Excited in the Soul; the Good, That
they May be Admitted; the Bad, That They May be Rejected: and These Rules are More Suitable for the First
Week.

Rules for the Same Effect, Containing a Fuller Discernment of Spirits, and More Suitable to the Second Week.

Rules for the Distribution of Alms: In the Ministry of
Distributing Alms the Following Rules are to be
Observed.

Rules on Scruples. The Following Notes Will be of Use
for Discerning and Understanding Scruples and the In-
sinuations of the Enemy.

Rules for Thinking with the Church. In Order to Know
Rightly What We Ought to Hold in the Church Militant,
the Following Rules Are to be Observed.

In the thirteenth of these last rules for thinking with the
Church, he has been condemned for saying that, if the Church
tells us that white is black, we must agree it is so. St. Ignatius is
not irrational. He says that, if what *seems* to us to be white is
declared by the Church to be black, we must conform our judgment. It is more reasonable to think that we are in error
than to ascribe error to the Holy Spirit of God ruling
and guiding the Church in the way of truth. Had St. Ignatius
said that we must believe what *is* in reality white to be in reality

black if the Church so orders, he would be indulging in foolish exaggeration; but that is precisely what he does not say.

Perhaps I cannot close this chapter, which tries to give an epitome of a little book, almost itself an epitome, more effectively than by quoting the last paragraph. It should serve to straighten out a tangled mental condition of the modern mind: "Although it is above all things praiseworthy to greatly serve God our Lord out of pure love, yet we ought greatly to praise the fear of His Divine Majesty, because not only is filial fear a pious and most holy thing, but even servile fear, when one cannot rise to anything better and more useful, is of great help to him to escape from mortal sin; and, after he has escaped from it, he easily attains to filial fear, which is altogether acceptable and pleasing to God our Lord, because it is inseparable from Divine love."

It must be remembered that, in the intention of the Saint, these exercises could be made in thirty days or three days, according to the capacity and disposition of the person or persons making them. Indeed, he provides for the case of a man who cannot find leisure for the Exercises, except in the evenings. Most of what are called "Missions" are exercises of this kind.

BIBLIOGRAPHY

FOR a summary history of the Jesuits, the reader is referred to the article by F. X. Talbot, S.J., in the *Encyclopaedia Brittanica* (Fourteenth Edition, Revised American Reprint), 1938. The Hastings *Encyclopaedia of Religion and Ethics,* 1924, has an excellent epitome by Herbert Thurston, S.J. The article on the Jesuits in the *Catholic Encyclopedia* is by J. H. Pollen, S.J. All these articles give important bibliographies. The bibliography appended to Theodore Maynard's *The Odyssey of Francis Xavier* (New York: Longmans, 1936) is notably extensive. *The Jesuits in Modern Times,* by J. La Farge, S.J. (New York: The America Press) treats of the contemporary Society.

Among lesser known *Lives* of Jesuit missionaries, which serve to illustrate the text, may be mentioned that of *Augustus Henry Law,* by Ellis Schreiber (London: Burns and Oates, 1893); and that of *Constant Lievens,* by Francis Joseph Bowen (Herder, 1937). Of the latter missionary, John A. Morrison, S.J., writes from Patna, India: "I have just returned from Ranchi. Father Lievens made Ranchi famous in mission history when he started a mass movement there a little over fifty years ago. He burnt out in only six years, but during that time seventy thousand were converted, and now there are three hundred thousand Catholics in the Ranchi Mission." *An American Missionary,* by Charles J. Judge, S.S. (New York: Maryknoll Press, 1907), is a sketch of Father Judge, S.J., by his Sulpician brother. Father Martin Carrabine, S.J., has written a pamphlet, based on Father Kane's memoir of William Stanton (New York: Jesuit Mission Press, 1932). *Arnold Damen, S.J.,* by Joseph P. Conroy, S.J. (St. Louis: Herder). Professor Frank C. Lockwood covers some of the ground of Professor Bolton in his paper, *With Padre Kino On the Trail* (University of Arizona Bulletin, Social Science Bulletin, No. 5). Father Garraghan's *The Jesuits in the Middle United States* (New York: America Press, 3 vols., 1938) gives numerous instances of missionary achievement.

The files of the *Revue d' Ascetique et de Mystique* and *La Vie Spirituelle* will yield abundant matter on the controversy over prayer. Father Joseph de Guibert, S.J., has a long article on Henri Bremond in the latter for July, 1937 (Vol. 1, col. 1928). Other works in French are *La Spiritualité Chrétienne,* by P. Pourrat, S.J., 4 vols. (Paris, 1917–1928). The first three volumes were published in English by Burns and Oates (1922–1927). *Des Grâces d'Oraison,* by A. Poulain, S.J. (Paris, 1901), appeared in English in 1912 under the title, *The Graces of Interior Prayer. Les Degrés de la Vie Spirituelle,* by A. Saudreau (Paris, 1896), was followed by other books on mysticism, most of them translated into English. *Perfectionne Chrétienne et Contemplation,* by R. Garrigou-Lagrange, has appeared in English, as well as his *Les Trois Voies de la Vie Spirituelle* (Burns and Oates, 1938). Lallement's *La Doctrine Spirituelle* is a classic work which has long been familiar in English dress. *Ascetica Ignatiana,* by Francesco Saverio Calcagno, is a Latin work in four volumes treating the subject of Ignatian spirituality, especially in the first volume (Rome: Marietti, 1936).

Original books in English on prayer are numerous. Besides those mentioned in the text, Archbishop Goodier's *Introduction to Ascetical and Mystical Theology* (Burns and Oates, 1938) is an interesting survey. Also, *Western Mysticism,* second edition, and *Ways of Christian Life,* by Dom Butler (Sheed and Ward, 1932) and *The Doctrine of Spiritual Perfection,* by Anselm Stoltz, O.S.B. (Herder). The devotional treatises of R. H. J. Steuart, S.J., have been popular spiritual books. *Merry in God,* a Life of William Doyle, by an intimate friend, who chooses to remain anonymous (Longmans, 1939), is a good companion memoir for Alfred O'Rahilly's.

Those readers who wish to know more about the Jesuit theory of education may find information in the following works: *Jesuit Code of Liberal Education,* by Allan Peter Farrell, S.J. (The Bruce Pub. Co., 1938); *Jesuits and Education* (Bruce, 1932) and *Catholic Way in Education* (Bruce, 1934), by William Joseph McGucken, S.J.; *Principles of Jesuit Education in Practice* (Kenedy, 1934), and *Literary Art and Modern Education* (Kenedy, 1927), by Francis P. Donnelly, S.J. *Essay Towards a History of Education* (Loyola Press, 1935) and *Some Principles of Education* (Loyola Press, 1938), by William T. Kane, S.J.